BETWEEN
THE LINES

43-OEHM

BETWEEN THE LINES

Reflections on the Gospels Through the Church Year

H. King Oehmig

An Anders Literary Group Book
P.O. Box 277
Winchester, TN 37398
piander@edge.net

Library of Congress Number: 98-88296
ISBN#:   Hardcover   0-7388-0153-4
                  Softcover   0-7388-0154-2

Published by special arrangement with Pasha Publications and Sedgwick
Publishing Co., P.O. Box 328, Boyds, MD 20841

This book was printed in the United States of America.

To order additional copies of this book, contact:
Xlibris Corporation   1-888-7-XLIBRIS
PO Box 2199   1-609-278-0075
Princeton, NJ 08543-2199   www.Xlibris.com
USA   Orders@Xlibris.com

CONTENTS

TO MARGY AND MARY

Introduction

What does it mean in a high-tech, low-touch world to lose your life in order to save it?

What does it mean for us—whose perceptions of reality are largely determined by science—to hear of Jesus' raising his friend Lazarus following a four-day death?

What does it mean in our world, predicated on advancement and achievement, when Jesus says that the last will be first and the first will be last?

What does it mean on Main Street or Wall Street that Jesus said, "take up your cross and follow me"?

To these situations, Scripture must speak in order to be a *living* Word. Not the preacher's Word, or a stained-glass Word, or a Word for the professionally religious. But a Word for us all, wherever we live and move and have our being.

As old St. Ambrose said, "As in Paradise, God walks in the Holy Scriptures, seeking us." So Scripture becomes an animated Word whenever we allow it to penetrate the hard shell of our "security systems," and to engage us. When this happens, the seeking God lifts us, confronts us, comforts us, and confuses us. The Holy Word beckons and baffles, and refuses to be domesticated. Like God, it will be what it will be.

The fiction writer Flannery O'Connor once commented on her use of the "grotesque" in her stories by saying: "To the hard of hearing you shout; to the blind you draw large and startling figures." And Jesus often did the same thing in his acts of healing, in the telling of parables, and in going to the Cross as a kind of parable in itself. He knew, as the writers of the Gospels knew, that we worldlings need to be shouted at. We need large and startling pictures drawn for us if the Old Creation is to crumble and make way for the New Creation we are meant to be.

In *Between the Lines: Reflections on the Gospels Through the Church Year,* I have sought to remind us that Scripture is a living Word of the Living God. What matters is not just what the Scripture *said,* but also what it *says.*

The Church's wisdom says that in order to know Jesus as the Living Word, we need to follow him down the path provided for in the Lectionary. This "wheel of Scripture" leads the people of God through a disciplined exposure to God's saving work, from the Advent of Jesus' Birth, through the Epiphany of his Revealing, on into the Season of Lent ... and to the joy of Easter. By reading "between the lines," we go on to experience his Ascension, the Feast of Pentecost, Trinity Sunday—and Lessons of the Church season known as "Ordinary Time" ... leading to Christ the King Sunday, at the end of the Church Year.

Throughout these reflections, it is my fervent hope that you will see Scripture afresh; that you will hear it as a contemporary Word as well as an ancient Word. My prayer is that you will begin to hear the written Word as a vehicle through which Jesus, the living Word, grasps you and lifts you into the reality of the Real.

In other words, *may you fall more deeply in love with God by reading what lies ahead.* May you discover, or rekindle, your own love affair with the Divine, and allow this love to become more nearly the sacred heartbeat of your life. If this happens, even in just a tiny, mustard-seed kind of way, we all shall be blessed.

Lastly, may these reflections build up your faith so that you can continue on your spiritual journey with greater wisdom and gentleness. May they draw you into God's abiding love, and, in turn, make you more of a Divine lover—a Gospel lover—best described by Desmond Tutu in his work *The Compassionate Church:*

> "A compassionate Church would remind people
> that they count, they matter enormously to God.
> Their worth is intrinsic to who they are. It comes

with the package of being human. They are of infinite value not because of anything extraneous, either biological achievement or any other attribute. They matter because God loves them. God loves them not because they are lovable; no, they are lovable because God loves them with a love that does not change; their names are engraved in the palms of his hand."

I pray that something of this realization might accompany you, the reader, through these scriptural meditations as you search *Between the Lines.*

H. King Oehmig
Chattanooga, Tennessee
Feast of the Transfiguration, 1998

1. Beyond the "Second Genesis"

Mark 13:(24-32) 33-37

Jesus said, ²⁴*"But in those days, after that suffering, the sun will be darkened, and the moon will not give its light,* ²⁵*and the stars will be falling from heaven, and the powers in the heavens will be shaken.* ²⁶*Then they will see the 'Son of Man coming in clouds' with great power and glory.* ²⁷*Then he will send out the angels, and gather his elect from the four winds, from the ends of the earth to the ends of heaven.* ²⁸*From the fig tree learn its lesson: as soon as its branch becomes tender and puts forth its leaves, you know that summer is near.* ²⁹*So also, when you see these things taking place, you know that he is near, at the very gates.* ³⁰*Truly I tell you, this generation will not pass away until all these things have taken place.* ³¹*Heaven and earth will pass away, but my words will not pass away.* ³²*But of that day or hour no one knows, neither the angels in heaven, nor the Son, but only the Father.* ³³*Beware, keep alert; for you do not know when the time will come.* ³⁴*It is like a man going on a journey, when he leaves home and puts his slaves in charge, each with his work, and commands the doorkeeper to be on the watch.* ³⁵*Therefore, keep awake—for you do not know when the master of the house will come, in the evening, or at midnight, or at cockcrow, or at dawn,* ³⁶*or else he may find you asleep when he comes suddenly.* ³⁷*And what I say to you I say to all: Keep awake."*

I.   The "young and bombarded."

In an article from *Leadership* magazine entitled "Brain Scan of America: Reading the Minds of Today's Listeners," contributing editor Craig Brian Larson talked with Michael Sack, the president and CEO of Quali-Quant Research, Inc., a research and marketing firm that serves several Fortune 500 companies, as well as various Christian organizations.

When asked how communicating with the "American mind" has changed since 1950, Sack said that today young people see almost 1,000% more images than 55-year-olds witnessed in their youth (as to Generation Xers, from ages 16-25, the media are hitting them with about *2,000* images a day). The impact of this on communicating the Gospel is that the ability to find meaning in print or video is much greater for those over 50 than it is for every younger generation. These older folks have been far less bombarded with this mighty stream of images; hence, they are still impressionable. They can savor—take in and emotionally connect with—many of the images they see.

For the "young and bombarded," however, being flashed with so many images on a daily basis lessens the emotional impact an image carries. Sack says that the younger the person, the harder it is to convey meaning or moral value to him or her through images. That is because these younger folk have become adept at handling image overload. They ignore most of the images. The ones that they do connect with are received because of color or movement—for entertainment value. "The young," Sack says, "eat images like popcorn; older adults eat them like a meal."

In order to find out what Americans believed in, Sack gave thousands of people pictures and asked them to create a collage that would symbolically reveal the "God they believed in" and the "God they didn't believe in." Not surprisingly, for the boomers on down, "the God they didn't believe in" revolved around images of discomfort. The idea of evil, or of sin-induced suffering, had been edited out of their theology—and out of their lives. (Was this one of the side-effects of "political correctness" on the "boomer" generation on down—the tendency to consider all ideas and all beliefs equally?—Sack wondered.)

To make his point, Sack gave an example of what happened to

him and his associate on a business trip to Manila. A common sight in the streets of Manila is for a diseased child to crawl up to the side window of a car waiting in traffic and start begging—to plead with the occupants to have mercy, and to spare some small offering so the child can at least eat that day. When some of these disheveled, diseased children came up to their car, Sack said that his associate—middle-class and suburban—went rigid. He could not look at the children. He could not look into their eyes of suffering—into the world's unspeakable, unredeemed pain. Into anything "negative." He asked the driver to "hurry up."

II. The "second genesis" of the world.

Is it any wonder then that the framers of the Lectionary for this First Sunday of Advent make optional verses 24-32 of Mark 13? Is there any doubt why they are ambivalent about bringing up for view, in our preference for sweetness and light, images of a world in wholesale collapse, a cosmos caught up in the "great tribulation," a world in which "the sun will be darkened, and the moon will not give its light, and the stars will be falling from heaven, and the powers in the heavens will be shaken" (vv. 24-25)? Like the guy in Manila, or the Xer in front of MTV, we look the other way—or we rapaciously crunch the image before moving on to another fistful of popcorn.

That is why Advent tells us to be quiet. To be awake. To be sober and to still ourselves. Why? So that we can receive the truth, a truth that we have been socially constructed not to receive: the image of a world order that has no enduring value—not even in the most sacred religious institutions (cf. Mk. 13:2). The image of a future that is wholly foreign to our sense and sensibilities. A future that is completely out of our control, one that belongs entirely to God. The image of God's "second genesis" in Jesus Christ, in which all that we have known and relied on in the past is eclipsed in the twinkling of an eye.

Get quiet and heedful, the season of Advent tells us—like a child settling in to hear a bedside spellbinder. And then, hear about Jesus sitting on the Mount of Olives, across the Kidron Valley from Jerusalem, facing the temple. Hear how he reveals the terrible, yet tantalizing future, not to the crowds, but to his closest disciples—Andrew, Peter, James, and John. Hear about the false messiahs. Wars, and rumors of wars. Earthquakes. Famines. Hear of the persecutions, of the families being rent apart. Hear, finally, of the dissolute world giving way to the coming of the Son of Man "in clouds with great power and glory" (v. 26).

III. Revelation on Memorial Bridge.

The Rev. Dr. Albert Mollegen, who first began to teach Christian ethics at Virginia Theological Seminary in the 1930s, recalled in his book *Christianity and Modern Man: The Crisis of Secularism* (Indianapolis: Bobbs-Merrill Co., 1961) the popularity of "Christian Utopianism" at that time. "Molly" was questioning the realism of many who asserted that "the social gospel" could bring about the Kingdom "on earth as it was in heaven." He did not believe in "human progress" or that "every day, in every way, we are getting better and better." He used to say "a very hard word" to his seminarians—and to himself—about the illusion of the perfectibility of the world by human means.

To prove his point, the professor would ask his students to stand in the middle of Memorial Bridge over the Potomac, and look both ways—to the great monument of Abraham Lincoln on the Washington side of the river, and to Arlington Hall, the historic home of Robert E. Lee, on the other side of the river. After they had done this, "Molly" would ask his students to meditate on the fact that if, in the course of their ministry, they produced laity who were up to the character of Abraham Lincoln and Robert E. Lee, they could well congratulate themselves for having a good ministry under God. And yet these two "statesmen" had presided over what was then the bloodiest war in American history, a war in which over 500,000 people lost their lives.

Professor Mollegen's point in the exercise was to reveal the human tendency to resist idolatry with idolatry. This did not mean we were to abdicate what we should be doing as Christians in the world—in short, to do everything in our power to renew the world until the coming of Christ. What he meant was that whenever we look to a "final solution" in terms of this world—be it military, or economic, technological, or political—we have yielded to the force of self-deification. We have resisted idolatry with idolatry. We have missed the mark.

The New Testament ends with the prayer: "Amen. Come, Lord Jesus!" (Rev. 22:20). The prayer says it all: our hope for deliverance and perfection lies not with us, but with Christ. Jesus Christ alone is our security, our final and true dependability. Christ, who will come again to judge the living and the dead, will step through time into time, healing our past, inspiring our present, and consummating our bliss. Thanks be to God.

2. By "Accident" of Birth

Luke 1:26-38

26In the sixth month the angel Gabriel was sent by God to a town in Galilee called Nazareth, 27to a virgin engaged to a man whose name was Joseph, of the house of David. The virgin's name was Mary. 28And he came to her and said, "Greetings, favored one! The Lord is with you." 29But she was much perplexed by his words and pondered what sort of greeting this might be. 30The angel said to her, "Do not be afraid, Mary, for you have found favor with God. 31And now, you will conceive in your womb and bear a son, and you will name him Jesus. 32He will be great, and will be called the Son of the Most High, and the Lord God will give to him the throne of his ancestor David. 33He will reign over the house of Jacob forever, and of his kingdom there will be no end." 34Mary said to the angel, "How can this be, since I am a virgin?" 35The angel said to her, "The Holy Spirit will come upon you, and the power of the Most High will overshadow you; therefore the child to be born will be holy; he will be called Son of God. 36And now, your relative Elizabeth in her old age has also conceived a son; and this is the sixth month for her who was said to be barren. 37For nothing will be impossible with God." 38Then Mary said, "Here am I, the servant of the Lord; let it be with me according to your word." Then the angel departed from her.

I.   Luke alone tells how the "accident happened."

With the arrival of "Mary Sunday," we have reached the third trimester of Advent. The theme of expectation still fills the air, but no longer is it filled with an aroma of apocalyptic expectancy—such as the Son of Man returning to end human history and establish the unthwarted reign of God. No longer do we hear ringing in our ears John the Baptist's chastising us into wholesale repentance—and into looking for the one "coming after him," the one who will baptize, not with water, but with the fire of the Holy Ghost. By now, we should be awake, and should be focusing on Mary and her child.

When both of our children were born in Flowood, Mississippi, in the early 1980s, the health insurance forms read something like this: "Where did the accident happen? How did it occur? How many people were involved?" And of all the four evangelists who authored "Gospels" on the life of Jesus, only Luke had the nerve to tackle such insurance-like questions on the birth of Jesus. Mark simply never mentions it. Matthew treats it—but only on his way to emphasizing the more important visit of the Magi. John opts for the "cosmic treatment," locating Christ as the preexistent Word from before time—not as one who came to life in a cold cave reeking of animal dung and afterbirth in Bethlehem of Judea.

Only Luke takes the risk. Only Luke rolls up his sleeves—spending God-knows-how-many sleepless nights in front of his word processor—praying about how to describe what he never saw happen, in something like insurance-form precision. Since Luke was a doctor, maybe that is why God chose him for the job. And a daunting job it was. For you see, Joseph Campbell notwithstanding, this birth was different from other god-induced pregnancies known to the ancient world. It was not the same as the Greeks' saying that Plato had been the child of Perictone. Or that the Pharaohs' mothers had all been impregnated by the god Amon, who appeared to them in human form as a king. In each of these instances, no stress was laid on the virginity of the mother—each had had sexual intercourse with a god in human form.

But not so with Mary. And only Luke, blessed be he, took the great risk of telling the world in as much insurance-like detail as possible concerning the "scandal of the crib." He took the risk to tell the truth to a people who had lost faith, yet were at the same time desperately looking for it. To tell how timelessness and time intersected with particular people, in particular places, for a particular purpose—to weave together the tapestry of the Incarnation. To tell educated, skeptical Romans how the Divine and the human married in this mysterious event, and how God's deliverance of the world from evil began in the hidden encounter between an angel named Gabriel and an unwed, teenage mother named "Mary."

II. Mary: the archetype of the Church.

Luke's task in his day and our task as communicators of the Word today share a distinct commonality. We, too, address a "sophisticated" people who also are spiritually adrift. We speak to a world skeptical of faith, yet thirsting for it as well. That is why Luke's pattern of disclosure—centering the coming of Jesus in the person of Mary—should be our model of preparing our people for the birth of God. And what does Mary, as our "Mother in faith," teach us?

First, *she is completely herself.* There is nothing pretentious about her. There is nothing "extraordinary" in her life about which she could boast. There is nothing that would compel God's favor, nothing to make her qualified to receive a breath-stopping annunciation over other potential recipients. She hailed from Nazareth—an unimportant village in Galilee. She had no formal education. She held no high-powered job. When it came to organized religion, there was nothing distinct about her. Unlike notably religious men in her culture, it was never said of Mary that she occupied a prominent seat in the synagogue, or that she was one of the people to "stand and pray" at streetcorners. She didn't "sound a trumpet" while living her quiet, spiritual life.

To the contrary, Mary seems wholly content to be who she was. It is little wonder then that when she receives the angelic greeting and the news that she is favored by God, Mary doesn't break out in peals of "alleluias"; she is "perplexed" (v. 29). To the announcement that she will bear a son named Jesus, who will be called the "Son of the Most High" and who will occupy the "throne of David" (v. 32), the fresh-faced, greatly troubled young woman unhesitatingly asks: "How can this be, since I am a virgin?" (v. 34). How honest. How refreshing. Mary's example says that *we do not have to be somebody else for God to enter our lives with great significance.* We don't have to strive to gain favor with God. To try to be professionally religious, or to be an ascetic, or even a saint. We do, however, need to be open, which leads to the next point:

Second, even though it would mean scandal—having a child out of wedlock (who would later be executed as a criminal)—Mary courageously offers herself as the means of Christ's birth in the world anyway. It is heroic faith at its best. Saying "yes" to God when everything in your world shouts "no"—daring to enter this "cloud of unknowing"—is exemplary trust. In her trust, Mary models the risk-filled nature of a vocation dedicated to expressive faith. Meister Eckhart (1260—1327), the German Dominican mystic, once said: "We are all meant to be mothers of God, for God is always needing to be born." Mary, the *theotokos,* is therefore the prototype Christian—the one who, impregnated by the Holy Spirit, gives birth to Jesus in the world—despite the inevitable suffering that goes with it. Eckhart would proceed to say: "What good is it to me if Mary gave birth to the Son of God fourteen hundred years ago, and I do not also give birth to the Son of God in my time and in my culture?" The mystic's question remains as pertinent today as it was 700 years ago.

Third, Mary's response to Gabriel's announcement—"Here am I, the servant of the Lord; let it be with me according to your word" (v. 38)—*is totally unforced.* Gabriel places no compulsion on her response. She is not strong-armed into obedience—or else. She isn't threatened into saying yes, coerced to be faithful. Only Mary's *free acceptance* of the call—this willingness to trust at face value what was spoken to her by the angel—could turn the *possi-*

bility of the Incarnation into an *actuality*. And likewise, it is only our trust in God, freely turned into faith-in-action, that moves *latent faith* into *realized faith*.

Herbert O'Driscoll tells a story from his childhood in the south of Ireland that well illustrates this last point. One of the workers on his grandfather's farm, John Brennan, was a great storyteller. Many evenings the two of them would sit in front of the farmhouse, and Brennan would regale O'Driscoll with many wonderful tales, many of which would stay with him forever. One such, O'Driscoll distinctly remembers. Just as the first stars began to sparkle in the darkening sky, John Brennan said that it reminded him of the time when the angel Gabriel came to Mary and told her of her special vocation. After the angel gave Mary the announcement, but before her response, there ensued a long silence. In that silence, he said, all the suns and the planets and stars ceased to move. When Mary replied, "Let it be with me according to your word," the universe once again resumed motion.

3. What Are We Looking For?

Luke 2:1-14

¹In those days a decree went out from Emperor Augustus that all the world should be registered. ²This was the first registration and was taken while Quirinius was governor of Syria. ³All went to their own towns to be registered. ⁴Joseph also went from the town of Nazareth in Galilee to Judea, to the city of David called Bethlehem, because he was descended from the house and family of David. ⁵He went to be registered with Mary, to whom he was engaged and who was expecting a child. ⁶While they were there, the time came for her to deliver her child. ⁷And she gave birth to her firstborn son and wrapped him in bands of cloth, and laid him in a manger, because there was no place for them in the inn. ⁸In that region there were shepherds living in the fields, keeping watch over their flock by night. ⁹Then an angel of the Lord stood before them, and the glory of the Lord shone around them, and they were terrified. ¹⁰But the angel said to them, "Do not be afraid; for see—I am bringing you good news of great joy for all the people: ¹¹to you is born this day in the city of David a Savior, who is the Messiah, the Lord. ¹²This will be a sign for you: you will find a child wrapped in bands of cloth and lying in a manger." ¹³And suddenly there was with the angel a multitude of the heavenly host, praising God and saying, ¹⁴"Glory to God in the highest heaven, and on earth peace among those whom he favors!"

I. The three types of religion.

The noted Southern writer, Walker Percy, would often deal with a common theme in his modern fiction—the fulfillment, yet unfulfillment of those whom the world would consider "successful." This theme could well be represented in a scene in which a white-collar professional is commuting from work to her home in the suburbs. She has achieved all of her career goals. She has had an enduring, reasonable marriage. She and her husband have reared successful, responsible children—each primed to do successful things in the world. She has had many good friends and colleagues along the way. She has experienced an active social life. She drives a nice car. She has, in other words, fulfilled the "American dream." Yet, Percy asks, why does she look out the window and feel a terrible sadness? What is she looking for? *What are we looking for?*

The realm of religion has often been looked to at such times of "terrible sadness." And, in general, there are three types of religion that have sought to provide an answer. *The first* concerns what has been called the "religion of nature." In this type of religion, God, or one's "Higher Power" is discerned through the natural world. God is in Grape Nuts—or a macrobiotic diet. Or God is experienced in the brilliant auras of a breathless sunset. Or God can be discovered in the rational principle disclosed in a DNA molecule—or in the planets and stars set in their highly complex orbits. God is perceived in the quiet evolution of a tiger swallowtail from its home-spun cocoon. Or, God comes to be known through the mystery of seasonal change, in the recurring cycles of wintering and summering.

Then there is *the second,* the "religion of contemplation." In this form of religion, usually with deep ties to the East, the physical is perceived as illusory—and therefore is highly suspect. Woe is connected with the love of anything or anybody in the world. The good life is not found in this dimension; in fact, the good life serves as an impediment to enlightenment. The physical world is to be transcended. The world of the senses eschewed. Through contemplation, the aspirant in the religion of contemplation seeks union with the Divine, to transcend the physical bonds of time and place, of earthliness and history, and move into formlessness.

The third type of religion is the "religion of history." Simply put, in this kind of religion the Divine is made known through "mighty acts." It is a religion grounded in a common memory from which the present draws power—and hope becomes operative. It is a religion anchored *in* the world, not *out* of it. This is so because it is in the world that God chooses to be known, and *is* made known. God speaks in history, acts in history, and ultimately directs history to its intended fulfillment. Whether it is God saying, "Let there be light," or God calling Abraham and Sarah to leave Haran, or God summoning Moses to return to Egypt at the burning bush to "let my people go," there is self-revelation. This occurs also in God's giving of the Law to the Covenant people, in Isaiah's telling the Israelites they have whored after false gods, and in Persia's Cyrus defeating the Babylonians in 538 B. C., thereby ending the Babylonian Captivity. In all of these events, history is not seen as an absurdity, but as the medium containing God's defining self-disclosure.

II.   ... And a paradox in a pear tree.

Which brings us to this Silent Night, this Holy Night. We say rightly that God is present at all time and in all places. That God is somehow present in every moment. But there are some times— holy moments—in which "ordinary time" yields to "sacred time." Moments, even days when the Divine is more focused or concentrated than at other times. Through such a time you can catch a glimpse of eternity. And this night stands uniquely in sacred time as the most sacred of all. The night when the womb of history brings forth an event without precedent—yet an event that had no recorded date, and which for more than 100 years was never mentioned by a Roman historian. The night, unlike any other night before or since, when God not only *acted* in history, but *entered* history. Not as a voice. Not in a bush that would not burn up, not in tablets of stone, not in a cloud. Not in a whirlwind. Not in a prophet, a priest, a judge, or a king. Not in an angel. Not in deep meditation. Not in a sermon or a spiritual feeling. But as one of us. The enfleshment of God. Emmanuel.

And yet, even though we Christians claim the birth of Jesus as God's decisive entry into history, the event itself remains forever paradoxical. This holy night which at once causes heaven to rejoice, at the same time causes earth to reject. On this night in which angels sing, there is no room for an exhausted, expectant couple at the inn. On this night, when all the bigshots in the world go to sleep happy—Augustus in Rome; Quirinius in Syria; Pilate in Judea; Annas and Caiaphas in Jerusalem—simple shepherds, thought to be no better than thieves, are summoned as the only witnesses of the mystery of the ages, the birth of the "Savior," the "Wonderful Counselor," the "Prince of Peace."

Furthermore, it is an event hard to fathom—better left to the philosophers and theologians to argue about over cappuccino. To understand how Being itself becomes a being. How the "potentiality" of God becomes an "actuality" in a particular human being without making God seem less Godlike. The event in which the Highest Being enters human existence in the lowest place. Where the Unlimited has become limited. Where the Infinite has become finite. Where the Unknowable has become known. Where the Unnamable has become named. Where God—the Ineffable, the Unutterable Ground of all Being and Lord of history—is enfleshed in a neonate cradled in the feedbox of a donkey.

III. The birth of Christianity at Caesarea Philippi, not in Bethlehem of Judea.

Paul Tillich maintained that Christianity was born, not with the birth of the infant Jesus, but when his followers came to the conclusion, "You are the Christ" (Mk. 8:29). The earliest disciples, in other words, did not follow Jesus because he was born of a virgin, or because they knew of his miraculous birth. It was only after they had been with Jesus—had lived with him, listened to him, and experienced the power of God in him—that they could affirm his divinity.

That being the case, the real manger on Christmas Eve is the human heart. That is where the "Christ" of Christmas is known to be real and true—not where Jesus lies in a manger with a special star overhead. It means, however, that Bethlehem is no less true than other events in the life of Jesus in Capernaum or in Caesarea Philippi or at Golgotha. Because we have experienced him as the one who brings the New Creation, we kneel in awe and wonder and praise this night. Because we have found in Jesus Christ God's ultimate love, God's whole-making power to defeat sin and death, we surrender our lives in faith to the one whom the shepherds adore. And because we have found in Jesus Christ the New Birth, we join with the heavenly hosts singing: "Glory to God in the highest heaven, and on earth peace among those whom he favors!" (Lk. 2:14).

4. God Up Close and Personal

Luke 3:15-16, 21-22

¹⁵As the people were filled with expectation, and all were questioning in their hearts concerning John, whether he might be the Messiah, ¹⁶John answered all of them by saying, "I baptize you with water; but one who is more powerful than I is coming; I am not worthy to untie the thong of his sandals. He will baptize you with the Holy Spirit and fire." ²¹Now when all the people were baptized, and when Jesus also had been baptized and was praying, the heaven was opened, ²²and the Holy Spirit descended upon him in bodily form like a dove. And a voice came from heaven, "You are my Son, the Beloved; with you I am well pleased."

I. Pascal's "definitive conversion."

"Can we actually 'know' the universe?" Woody Allen asked. And then, before anyone could attempt an answer, he said, "It's hard enough finding your way around Chinatown." Either looking through a telescope, or reading the street signs in Chinatown, the question of Epiphany is Woody Allen's question: "Can we actually 'know' the universe?" Or, one step further, can we know the God of the universe—at least in any way that matters to us?

The renowned French scientist/mathematician Blaise Pascal (1623—1662) underwent what he called a "definitive" conversion experience on November 23, 1654. As a testimony to his change of heart, and the new way he had come to know God, Pascal sewed into the lining of his favorite coat the following words:

"Not the God of the philosophers nor the God of science, but the God of Abraham, Isaac, and Jacob."

Pascal, in his conversion experience, could easily be the poster child for the season of Epiphany. For the self-disclosure of God, Pascal learned, as testified to by the statement stitched in his jacket, was that the One who converted him was far from the "remote" God of the philosophers. This was not an aloof God—nor a purely cerebral God either. This was not a God detached from human concern, who lived only in the realm of concepts and theories. A God who could best be apprehended by reason—mathematically or propositionally. One, in fact, gets the feeling that Pascal had had enough of knowing this "Uncaused First Cause," this "Governor of the Universe," or this "Unmoved Mover." He needed more; a God to whom he could give his heart, as well as his head.

Pascal, like most of us non-savants, needed a personal, saving God. A God who was more than "pure Actuality." A God less apprehended by reason than by faith. In other words, Pascal needed a God who not only cared for him, but a God who would go to any length to make that care for humanity known—personally. A God whose self-risk and self-expenditure could be discerned in *history*, not simply contemplated under a microscope, or figured out in a mathematical equation.

Pascal's conversion led him to a God of *faith*, a God primarily of *relationship*. The God who called Abraham and Sarah to leave Haran—with no maps, and without any guarantees. This was the God who struggled with Jacob in the darkness at the Jabbok, so that Jacob might be changed into "Israel." This was the God who burned in a bush before Moses. The God who fingered this obscure shepherd (not to mention a felon and a lousy speaker), to return to Egypt and undo Pharaoh's tyrannical system of rule—the strongest in the world.

Pascal's God was the God who strengthened David, a pretty shepherd boy, to go out and fell the Philistine monster, Goliath. This was the God, surrounded by winged seraphs in the temple calling out "Holy, Holy, Holy," who made young Isaiah quake with unworthiness. The One who called Jeremiah from before he was formed in his mother's womb to be a prophet to the nations. Alas, this was not only a "God of the universe," but a God who could help you find your way through Chinatown, too.

II. Not a Cape Canaveral God.

This was the God of Jesus. And this is the God who appears to us—every first Sunday after the Epiphany—not in a formula, or through a high-tech microscope, but in the earthiness of a mystical rendezvous between a wilderness holy man, John, and his questing cousin, Jesus. This is "epiphany" at its biblical best. A God revealed up close and personal—if not "in your face." This is not a God beyond life—confined to the realm of "spirit"—but an enfleshed God, wholly concerned with healing the world of "matter," because matter matters.

This is Pascal's "new God." A God who from the heavens is definitively disclosed on *a river bank;* in a *cleansing rite of eschatological purification* that will inaugurate the Divine deliverance of the world by *the life and death of this man Jesus.* This is definitely not the same revelation of God you would imagine through the Hubbell telescope, or in a strand of DNA under an electron microscope, or the one that the Russian cosmonaut claimed to see while orbiting the earth. This is not a Cape Canaveral God, but a God bumped along in the womb as his mother rode a donkey to Bethlehem—who suckled at Mary's breast, who practiced a carpenter's trade that he learned from his father Joseph, and who grew up with his brothers and sisters in a little village named Nazareth. A God who suffered and died as a public spectacle, and who rose from the dead.

This is the God into whose arms we abandon ourselves in baptism. The One to whom we entrust our lives, and the One into whom we die—to live as Divine servants of Christ. The One who reaches us and grasps us and drowns us in Divine Love—the ongoing "epiphany" that baptism manifests and celebrates. This may be the God of the philosophers, and may be the God of the scientists, too. But it is assuredly the God of Abraham, Isaac, and Jacob.

III. "A baptism I will always remember and need to recount."

The Rev. Dr. John H. Westerhoff tells a profound story about a baptism that he witnessed some years ago in a small church outside Buenos Aires. This story makes the point about the God who calls not just for contemplation, but for new birth (from *Holy Baptism: A Guide for Parents and Godparents,* St. Luke's Episcopal Church, Atlanta, Georgia).

"As I walked in a bit late, I witnessed a congregation on its knees singing a Good Friday hymn. Down the aisle came a father carrying a handmade child's coffin. His wife carried a pail of water from the family well. Behind them came the godparents carrying a naked baby in a serape. With tears in his eyes the father put the coffin on the altar, the mother poured in the water, and the godparents handed the child over to the priest.

"As the priest asked the parents and godparents the required questions, he put the oil used in the last rites of the church on the child's skin. He took the baby and, holding its nose, immersed the child in the coffin with the words, 'You are drowned in the name of the Father and the Son and the Holy Spirit.' As he raised the child out of the water the child cried out as he probably had when he emerged from his mother's womb at his first birth.

"The priest held up the child and exclaimed, 'And you are resurrected that you might love and serve the Lord.' The congregation leaped up and began to sing an Easter hymn. The priest poured a perfumed oil over the child and, as he signed the baby with the cross, said, 'I now brand you, as we do cattle on the range, with the sign of the cross, so that the world will always know and you will never be able to deny to whom you belong.' The congregation broke into applause and came forward to offer the child the kiss of peace with the words, 'Welcome Juan Carlos

Christiano.' No longer was the child to be known as Juan Carlos Renosa. He had been adopted by and brought into a new family—the family called Christian. That was a baptism I will always remember and need to recount."

5. Jesus the Winemaker

John 2:1-11

¹On the third day there was a wedding in Cana of Galilee, and the mother of Jesus was there. ²Jesus and his disciples had also been invited to the wedding. ³When the wine gave out, the mother of Jesus said to him, "They have no wine." ⁴And Jesus said to her, "Woman, what concern is that to you and to me? My hour has not yet come." ⁵His mother said to the servants, "Do whatever he tells you." ⁶Now standing there were six stone water jars for the Jewish rites of purification, each holding twenty or thirty gallons. ⁷Jesus said to them, "Fill the jars with water." And they filled them up to the brim. ⁸He said to them, "Now draw some out, and take it to the chief steward." So they took it. ⁹When the steward tasted the water that had become wine, and did not know where it came from (though the servants who had drawn the water knew), the steward called the bridegroom ¹⁰and said to him, "Everyone serves the good wine first, and then the inferior wine after the guests have become drunk. But you have kept the good wine until now." ¹¹Jesus did this, the first of his signs, in Cana of Galilee, and revealed his glory; and his disciples believed in him.

I.   The obvious and the symbolic.

There are a couple of ways to view the miracles of Jesus—aside from the obvious choice of "belief" or "disbelief." One is the "sensory" way, the literal way. A great windstorm whips up waves that begin to swamp the disciples' boat one stormy night on Lake Galilee. More than a little panic-stricken, the disciples rouse Jesus, who is asleep on a cushion in the stern. Before Jesus rubs the sleep out of his eyes, he rebukes the wind, and then tells the sea to calm down. After the winds cease, and the sea turns to glass, Jesus chides the disciples for their fear, or "little faith." The story ends with the disciples breathless with awe at the mighty act, and speculating among themselves as to who Jesus could be for accomplishing such a mighty work (Mk. 4:35-41).

From the vantage point of the "sensory," what you read is what you get. Jesus did this, and the disciples did that. Period. But there is also another way to view the miraculous event—to see it as a "sign." To view what happened in the miracle not only from the point of view of the literal, but also from the point of view of the symbolic or figurative. Applied to the miracle of the stilling of the storm, it is clear that Jesus not only saved his close friends and himself from drowning that stormy night on the lake. He also, through the mighty act, displayed his messianic "lordship over nature." No ordinary mortal could do this; only God's Son, the Beloved.

II. What would Julia Child have said?

The same methods can be applied to the miracle at the wedding in Cana of Galilee. "On the third day," John says, Jesus and his disciples arrive at a wedding to which they have been invited. On the literal level, everyone can "see" the event. The receiving line extends out the door of the bride's home. The giddy couple receives arriving guests, who make sure to sign the book as they enter. The bridesmaids, already into the wine, lift their glasses high over their bouquets to toast the new couple as a photographer takes their picture. The parents of the groom and bride proudly hug all their relatives and guests. The local rabbi, who stayed back at the synagogue to sign the register and make sure the marriage contract was correct, is the last to arrive at the bride's home. Many stop to tell him what a beautiful service it was. His impatient wife appears mildly annoyed by the litany of praise.

The local caterer hovers over the servers to make sure that the trays of finger food and sliced fillet and the fruit plates are all full. Of particular concern to the caterer is that the wine flows freely— and fully. Abundant moments call for abundance, the caterer tells the kitchen staff, and then cites Ben Sirach, who declared that the "blood of the grape" was one of God's good things created for good people (39:25, 26). The whole wedding party—including Jesus and his disciples—agree wholeheartedly. By their uninhibited partying, the message is clear: "Let the good times roll!"

The band starts, the cake is cut, and the dancing begins. The wine is swilled and swilled. The good times do roll. Until the unthinkable happens. A host's worst nightmare. Julia Child's biggest "No-No." A successful caterer's swan song. The wine *gives out.* By now, all the liquor stores and supermarkets are closed. Fed Ex won't deliver until the morning. The humorist/playwright George Ade's dictum about weddings seems near the truth: "If it weren't for the presents, an elopement would be preferable."

But Mary, blessed be she, springs into action, and calls Jesus to task—even though his "time" has not yet come. *Son, take care of the wine.* And so Jesus, not without some resistance, proceeds to save the wedding—and probably the marriage—by turning six stone jars full of water into enough wine to turn the heads of Ernest or Julio Gallo.

III. A "sign" for our times.

"Jesus did this, the first of his signs, in Cana of Galilee, and revealed his glory; and his disciples believed in him," John says (v. 11)—which means that Jesus not only saved a party, he also proclaimed a Gospel that day in Cana. More than water was turned into wine, the signs say. An old mode of being gave way to a new mode of being. The Gospel of "new wine" was disclosed, and with this disclosure, certain truths became clear.

Upon inviting Jesus into your midst, the more miraculous life becomes. This does not mean that once you experience the "new wine" of Jesus' presence you will go around bending spoons or making unerring psychic predictions. And you'll still probably have to buy your wine at the grocery store—not to mention continuing to walk on land, and not on water. But you *will* experience the giftedness of the Holy Spirit, the effects of which Paul cites in 1 Corinthians 12:1-11, the Epistle for today. This giftedness is the active fermentation of the "new wine" in the life of the believer and the believing community.

The more jar-like I become, the more the new wine takes hold. The more centered in prayer I am, the more disciplined I am in worship and study and service, and the more available I am to be a vessel of the Spirit's power. When I continually create a place for the "water of my old way of life" to be transformed into the new wine of the Kingdom of God, I experience more deeply the Gospel Jesus brings.

I begin to marvel at the Spirit's "fermentation process" that starts to take hold in me. I see the strange and wonderful ways Gospel giftedness happens. I witness the abundance of God poured out of me for the sake of others. "Create a beautiful garden," a Chinese saying goes, "and the birds will come"—and something of the same truth happens when we become a "jar" for the Holy Spirit. Receptivity leads to release.

The more I am involved with the world, and in the world, the better the "new wine" becomes. It seems that the more one learns to live in the "flow" of God's giftedness—should we say, in "following one's bliss"—the more one becomes the living mystery that God wants us all to be. The new wine reaches even finer levels of taste and texture. Less and less do we desire to be the old wine that means living somebody else's life. Less and less do we desire to be "conformed to this world," to be caught up in a deadly "spirit of sameness." We are guided and we gravitate toward authenticity. We bear fruit, fresh fruit—often that we never imagined we would bear on our own.

W. H. Auden said that the "artist" is one who makes, while the "apostle" is one with a message. In living the gifted life of the Spirit, both the "artist" and the "apostle" come together. In the story of the miracle at Cana in Galilee, they unite in Jesus, the "artist and apostle" of the Gospel. By the Spirit of God, we too should become the artists and apostles—poured out new wine— for a world that continually needs a fresh supply.

6. "We Dance"

Mark 9:2-9

²After six days, Jesus took with him Peter and James and John, and led them up a high mountain apart, by themselves. And he was transfigured before them, ³and his clothes became dazzling white, such as no one on earth could bleach them. ⁴And there appeared to them Elijah with Moses, who were talking with Jesus. ⁵Then Peter said to Jesus, "Rabbi, it is good for us to be here; let us make three dwellings, one for you, one for Moses, and one for Elijah."⁶He did not know what to say, for they were terrified. ⁷Then a cloud overshadowed them, and from the cloud there came a voice, "This is my Son, the Beloved; listen to him!"⁸Suddenly when they looked around, they saw no one with them any more, but only Jesus. ⁹As they were coming down the mountain, he ordered them to tell no one about what they had seen, until after the Son of Man had risen from the dead.

I.   The power of myth.

In reflecting on the time spent in interviewing Joseph Campbell, for what came to be known as *The Power of Myth*, Bill Moyers told the following story, one of Campbell's favorites:

"In Japan for an international conference on religion, Campbell overheard another American delegate, a social philosopher from New York, say to a Shinto priest, 'We've been now to a good many ceremonies and have seen quite a few of your shrines. But I don't get your ideology. I don't get your theology.' The Japanese paused as though in deep thought and then slowly shook his head. 'I think we don't have ideology,' he said. 'We don't have theology. We dance.'"

On this Last Sunday in Epiphany, we walk with Jesus, Peter, James, and John up the "high mountain," which may well have been Mount Tabor or Mount Hermon; but, for Mark, it could have been any mountain. Location, or naming the place, was not important. Only what happened. And what happened transcended ideology or theology. It superseded dogma and doctrine. It went beyond buildings and budgets and bazaars. Committees and canvasses. Beyond arguing over the authority of Scripture, or who has the right to be ordained, or who can marry whom. It transcended, in other words, religious ideology or theology. Canon, Creed, and Clergy, all of them, compared to the glory of this moment, seemed like straw.

What happened on that unnamed mountain—a peak from which they could look back at the springlike Galilean ministry, and then forward to the winter of Calvary—was a dance. The Dance. An improvisational, magical dance between the Holy One Jesus called "Abba" and "the Beloved Son" caught up in the symphony of the Holy Spirit—witnessed by Elijah and Moses, and three astonished disciples. Rather than building booths when the dance ended, they should have just clapped.

II. The recovery of Gospel astonishment.

Robert Farrar Capon, in his work *The Astonished Heart: Reclaiming the Good News from the Lost-and-Found of Church History* (Grand Rapids: Eerdmans, 1996), says that the Church in our age suffers from an "utterly crippling disability." Composed of all kinds of competing ideologies and agendas, the Body is bereft of what Capon calls "Gospel-centered astonishment"—just exactly the kind of astonishment that filled the air on the Mount of Transfiguration. We all seem to have boarded one of the ideological buses running inside everybody's church—conservatives, moderates, and liberals. Furthermore, there are new buses pulling up to the curb all the time: "liberal Baptists, white-wine Methodists, fundamentalist Anglicans, High Church Lutherans, and Low Church Roman Catholics."

Capon points out that one of the rules of history is "that another bus will always be along soon." Ideological fads will come and go—and their ridership with them. What alone is the "taproot" of Christian enthusiasm—and also of Christian intellectualism—is *being astonished by the Gospel.* "We have forfeited *that fascination with strangeness* which alone can enable us to do justice to the strange God of the strange Scriptures whom we, as the strangest of all possible religious institutions, must represent to the world," Capon insists. We need to recover, he says, "the coin of astonishment."

The Church is the sacrament of God's presence in the world—or should be. And the heart of this sacramentality is the experience of the Holy One through Jesus Christ. The soul thirsts for transfiguration, to have communion with the Mystery that underlies and holds together all of existence. To go past the "bus thing." To go beyond carpools and careers. To transcend technology and trend charts. To go deeper than bulletin boards and business plans. To soar over ideology, or theology.

Meister Eckhart, the 13th-century mystic, may have said it best: "The ultimate and highest leave taking is leaving God for God." Leaving, in other words, the god created in our own image and likeness, and experiencing the God beyond concepts and notions. The God who is more than our constructs and consciences and categories and conduct. The God who is Wholly Other, and yet Unfailingly Present. The God made flesh in Jesus—and in us through the Holy Spirit.

III. Transfiguration happens.

So how do we get there? How do we not only behold the transfigured Christ on the mountain, but experience our own personal transfiguration? How do we become astonished by the Gospel—without becoming tent-erectors in the process? Worship. Service. Fellowship. Yes, of course. But there is more.

The Hasidic master, Rebbe Nachman of Breslov (1772—1810), counseled his followers: "Most of all, prayer is the gate through which we enter to God. Learn to pray and you'll come to know and be attached to the Holy One." As to how to pray, the Rebbe said this: "Talk to God as you would talk to your very best friend. Tell the Holy One everything." This is as good a place as any to start. With your inmost thoughts and feelings, express yourself fully to God—in the most open, unfeigned, unstrained way. If nothing "happens"—the Voice doesn't rumble, or a cloud doesn't appear—don't fret it. The Rebbe says that "just wanting to speak with God is in itself a very great thing."

Just keep at it. Pray from the heart like a child. Pray for the Light. Through the imagination of the heart, see yourself surrounded in the luminescence of the Holy Spirit—along with those for whom you feel drawn to pray. See them, and you yourself, transfigured in Light, hearing the affirmation that sets the believer free from the tyranny of the world's approval-seeking: "You are my beloved child."

Little by little, we make progress. Sometimes this means going "backward" before going "forward." Spiritual growth is rarely linear. But if we ask, we will receive. If we seek, we will find. When we knock, it will be opened. That is the promise (Mt. 7:7-8). And sometimes transfigurations occur.

A friend recalls visiting Evelyn Underhill (1875—1941), the great teacher on the mystical life, at her Campden Square house in 1937, after one of her bad illnesses. She was seated facing a glowing fire. Her friend said: "As I entered she got up and turned around, looking so fragile that a puff of wind might blow her away, *but* light simply streamed from her face illumined with a radiant smile. One could feel there and then that one was in the presence of the Mystery of the Lord's Transfiguration, in one of the members of his mystical body. I myself never saw it repeated on any other later meeting. It told one not only of *herself,* but more of God and of his Mystical Body than all her work put together."

7. Renewed and Recommitted

Matthew 6:1-6, 16-21

Jesus said, [1]"Beware of practicing your piety before others in order to be seen by them; for then you have no reward from your Father in heaven. [2]So whenever you give alms, do not sound a trumpet before you, as the hypocrites do in the synagogues and in the streets, so that they may be praised by others. Truly I tell you, they have received their reward. [3]But when you give alms, do not let your left hand know what your right hand is doing, [4]so that your alms may be done in secret; and your Father who sees in secret will reward you. [5]And whenever you pray, do not be like the hypocrites; for they love to stand and pray in the synagogues and at the street corners, so that they may be seen by others. Truly I tell you, they have received their reward. [6]But whenever you pray, go into your room and shut the door and pray to your Father who is in secret; and your Father who sees in secret will reward you. [16]And whenever you fast, do not look dismal, like the hypocrites, for they disfigure their faces so as to show others that they are fasting. Truly I tell you, they have received their reward. [17]But when you fast, put oil on your head and wash your face, [18]so that your fasting may be seen not by others but by your Father who is in secret; and your Father who sees in secret will reward you. [19]Do not store up for yourselves treasures on earth, where moth and rust consume and where thieves break in and steal; [20]but store up for yourselves treasures in heaven, where neither moth nor rust consumes and where thieves do not break in and steal. [21]For where your treasure is, there your heart will be also."

I.   What's *Lent?*

In a wonderful compendium of ecclesiastical laughs, the Rev. J. Stephen Hines has put together a fabulous little book called *Easy on the Alleluias, Harry: A Collection of Episcopal Church Humor* (Cashiers Press: 1993). In the section entitled "Kids," the Rev. Chad Minifie submitted this vignette appropriate to Ash Wednesday, or the beginning of Lent:

Two young teenage boys are having a conversation. One looks at the other and announces, "I've decided to give up pot for Lent." The other replies, "What's that?" "You know," he says, "it's that stuff you roll into cigarettes, and you smoke, and it makes you high." To which his friend retorts, "I know what *pot* is, what's *Lent?*"

Admittedly, this is a strange day in our world, a world that revolves so much around what George MacDonald called "respectable selfishness." First, we don't eat. We fast—and not for health reasons either, but for spiritual ones. And that decision is very strange in our overeating, yet diet-crazed, weight-fixated, youth-obsessed culture.

Next, we leave our normal Wednesday patterns and places—homes, offices, or schools—to attend a religious observance that had its origins hundreds of years after the time of Jesus—and is never mentioned in Scripture.

And Ash Wednesday feels so medieval. This has nothing to do with its beginnings in Rome as a ceremonial way for public sinners to begin their penance in the 7th century, nor how it evolved into a rite of *general penance* somewhere between the 8th and 10th centuries. It has to do with the unabashed and irregular earthiness of it all. Those cold, black ashes—the remains of decomposing palm branches from the previous year's Holy Week—that lie hidden in the bottom of a bowl over which a priest signs a sacred blessing. Then, in a silence akin to death, the same priest imprints the ashes as a cross upon the people's foreheads, and prophesies the death sentence that all of us labor and travail under: "Remember that you are dust, and to dust you shall return."

Ash Wednesday is unnatural in other ways too. We are not invited to go into our individual closets and beat our breasts. We gather *as a community of public penitents,* professing before God and each other that we are anything but OK. More to the point, we profess our common wretchedness—a profession that takes place in the most foreign of postures, *on our knees.* We 'fess up. We own up to the reality that we have followed the "devices and desires" of our own hearts; and we confess to a deeper malaise still, one that is beyond anything we have in our own power to correct. That malaise, of course, is the power of sin and death, and our own powerlessness to overcome these "twin towers" of evil apart from Christ.

II. Repentance is about rebirth, not "deep gloom."

But just because Ash Wednesday has medieval and macabre elements to it, the rite should not dispirit us. As Rabbi Shlomo said: "The worst thing the Evil Urge can achieve is to make someone forget he is the son of a king." The liturgy should free, not depress, as God is not interested in guilt or despondency or "deep gloom"—only rebirth. The father of the Prodigal couldn't have cared less that his son had decided to come home for no more "noble" reason than to use him as a meal ticket.

And when the boy starts in on his carefully rehearsed confession—expertly designed to tug at his father's heart strings—the old man doesn't even hear it. That is because the important thing was not the purity of the boy's confession, but the fact that he had been *lost* and now was *found* (Lk. 15:17-24).

Besides, as Tony Campolo points out, "repentance" is not always understood for what it is. Campolo, the chairman of the Dept. of Sociology at Eastern College, had a friend who was falling out of love with his wife. He took the advice of another friend who suggested some ways to revive the marriage.

A few days later, Campolo got a phone call from the friend who had tried to make things right with his wife. Here's what happened:

"Every day I leave for work, put in a hard day, and come home tired and testy. I go to the refrigerator, get a beer, and then watch television until supper. After talking to my friend, I decided to make some changes. Before I left for work, I shaved and freshened up. On the way home, I stopped at a florist, and bought a bouquet of roses. Instead of going to the back door, I went to the front door and rang the doorbell.

"My wife opened the door, took one look at me, and started to cry. When I asked her what was wrong, she said, 'It's been a horrible day. First, Billy broke his foot and had to have it put in a cast. I no sooner get home from the hospital when your mother calls and tells me she is thinking about visiting us for three weeks. Then I try to wash some clothes and the #!** washing machine breaks, spewing water all over the basement—and now you have to come home drunk!'"

III. Out of the mouths of babes ...

So how should we leave the service today—besides with smeared ashes across our foreheads? Released? Yes. Reconfirmed? Yes. Recommitted? Yes. Renewed? Yes. And also reminded. Reminded that a new creation in Christ is the goal of all Lenten disciplines. Reminded of this truth by what Harvard psychologist Robert Coles found out from a nine-year-old girl, as quoted in *The New York Times Book Review* (Nov. 25, 1990):

"When you are put here, it's for a reason. The Lord wants you to do something. If you don't know what, then you've got to try hard to find out what. It may take time. You may make mistakes. But if you pray, He'll lead you to your direction. He won't hand you a piece of paper with a map on it, no sir. He'll whisper something, and at first you may not even hear, but if you have trust in Him and you keep turning to Him, it will be all right."

8. The Two Sides of Temptation

Luke 4:1-13

¹Jesus, full of the Holy Spirit, returned from the Jordan and was led by the Spirit in the wilderness, ²where for forty days he was tempted by the devil. He ate nothing at all during those days, and when they were over, he was famished. ³The devil said to him, "If you are the Son of God, command this stone to become a loaf of bread." ⁴Jesus answered him, "It is written, 'One does not live by bread alone.'" ⁵Then the devil led him up and showed him in an instant all the kingdoms of the world. ⁶And the devil said to him, "To you I will give their glory and all this authority; for it has been given over to me, and I give it to anyone I please. ⁷If you, then, will worship me, it will all be yours." ⁸Jesus answered him, "It is written, 'Worship the Lord your God, and serve only him.'" ⁹Then the devil took him to Jerusalem, and placed him on the pinnacle of the temple, saying to him, "If you are the Son of God, throw yourself down from here, ¹⁰for it is written, 'He will command his angels concerning you, to protect you,' ¹¹and 'On their hands they will bear you up, so that you will not dash your foot against a stone.'" ¹²Jesus answered him, "It is said, 'Do not put the Lord your God to the test.'" ¹³When the devil had finished every test, he departed from him until an opportune time.

I.   "Inner ripeness" and the desert experience.

Hindu literature contains a metaphor about a person's reaching a mature state of inner ripeness that signals a profound shift in life. Like growing up. The metaphor is expressed in the following way:

"When the young plant is just sprouting out of the seed, or is still weak and tender, it requires seclusion and the protection of a strong, thorny fence to keep off cattle that might otherwise eat it or trample upon it and destroy it.

"But the same shoot, when it develops into a large tree, dispenses with such protection and itself affords shade, sustenance, and protection to animals and humans alike, without detriment to itself."

The baptism of Jesus marked a watershed event in his life. It meant that Jesus had "sprouted." He had reached a point of "inner ripeness." No longer a "young plant ... weak and tender," Jesus had, by the time of his baptism, "increased in wisdom and in years, and in divine and human favor" (Lk. 2:52). He was ready to break out of the cocoon of a protected adolescence and assume his legitimate "treeness"—to afford shade, sustenance, and protection to a world that never was on record as asking for it.

With the "living water" of the Holy Spirit dripping off of him every bit as much as the Jordan River is rolling off his back, Jesus hardly has time to dry off before God presents him with a "maturing experience" extraordinaire. By the Spirit's power, Jesus is hurled off the Ponderosa of his youth and into the dark shadows of a Stephen King wasteland. He is driven into the abandoned land where the winds and wild beasts howl, where ordinary people fear to tread—not to mention angels. The desert is the place where evil spirits go to dwell (Mt. 12:43), and where the "Prince of demons" lays satanic traps. For Jesus, there is no more seclusion, no more protection—the war has broken out.

II. Two biblical notions of "temptation."

The notion of "temptation" in Scripture generally conveys two dominant understandings. The first is that of "testing." This understanding maintains that spiritual strength is proved by one's being put to the test—and then remaining faithful through the trial. One thinks of God's "testing" Abraham in the sacrifice of

Isaac (Gen. 22:1-19), or Job's undergoing tremendous "testing" to reveal the depth of his commitment to God through the terrible things that happen in his life (Job 1-7). In 1 Peter, the writer thinks of the persecution of Christians as a kind of "testing" that will ultimately lead to the community's developing greater devotion to Christ (1:3-9).

In the passing of these "tests," the people of faith are supposed to strengthen their character, and to enhance the depth of their commitment to God. The Apostle Paul, speaking as one who underwent many "tests"—from his famous "thorn in the flesh," to multiple calamities during his ministry (2 Cor. 11-12)—could honestly say to the church in Rome: "... suffering produces endurance, and endurance produces character, and character produces hope, and hope does not disappoint us, because God's love has been poured into our hearts through the Holy Spirit that has been given to us" (Rom. 5:3-5).

The second understanding of temptation has more to do with popular notions. The devil-made-me-do-it understanding of "temptation" denotes an enticement to sin that leads one away from God and from fidelity to one's neighbor. In this second notion, the writers of Scripture insist that God does not tempt human beings to do evil—anything but. In the Lord's Prayer, Jesus prays to the Father: "Do not bring us to the time of trial" (Mt. 6:13). The writer of James declares: "No one, when tempted, should say, 'I am being tempted by God'; for God cannot be tempted by evil and he himself tempts no one" (1:13).

To the contrary, in the New Testament, God provides the resources for us to resist or overcome temptation. Paul assures the church in Corinth: "God is faithful, and he will not let you be tested beyond your strength, but with the testing he will also provide the way out so that you may be able to endure it" (1 Cor. 10:13).

III. The psychology of temptation.

To sneak a chocolate sundae. To "hedge" a few line items on a tax return. To sleep with someone you know you are not supposed to. To gossip about another's life—especially his or her problems. To engage in the telling of innocent "white lies." To take to drinking or drugging or eating when you know these habits can dominate your life and lead to grave consequences. To keep silent when someone tells a racial or ethnic or sexist joke. To claim busyness when family members or loved ones need you. To sell out your personal values to meet the expectations of the "system." To hide behind "spirituality" as a way of avoiding earthly responsibilities. The list is endless. The possibility of doing good can only exist in the context of its shadow reality—the capacity to miss the mark. Without such a setup, there is no such thing as temptation. It's been that way from the start. No serpent, no apple—and Adam and Eve are still without clothes.

Dr. Rollo R. May in his work *The Art of Counseling* (Nashville: Abingdon, 1978) discusses what he calls the "psychology of temptation." His first point is that the psychology of temptation is not well understood by religious people, people who are long on exhortation and short on understanding. This lopsidedness leads to the "fish in the net" syndrome. That is, like fish caught in a net, the more people fight to get free of the temptation they resist, the more enmeshed in the "net" they become. Their last state is worse than the first. White-knuckling their way into "self-mastery," they get steamrolled by the forces of the unconscious, which mock such perfectionism. The "dark side" eventually erupts, and the ensuing volcano of unmanageability leads to intense feelings of guilt and a debilitating sense of worthlessness.

May contends that most temptations are not overcome by a direct "frontal" attack. In fact, especially in matters of desire, the more the "thou shalt not" is emphasized the more vivid the desire becomes, and the stronger the temptation gets. The best way to remove the power of temptation, May insists, is to remove the image from the center of one's attention, which is precisely what Jesus does with Satan. He does not deny or repress the temptations; rather, Jesus lifts them to a higher plane than "self-conquest." He yields them to God. He sees them in light of God's holy love, and within the context of God's call on his life—a messiahship of servant leadership. Jesus doesn't fight the satanic temptations by dwelling on them; he submits them to the power and grace of God. It is a power revealed in Scripture, and made operative through the Holy Spirit.

His "treeness" now proven, Jesus will emerge from the desert as the One in whom the divided state of the human will shall forever find victory. The New Adam has come.

9. One Day at a Time

Luke 13:1-9

¹At that very time there were some present who told Jesus about the Galileans whose blood Pilate had mingled with their sacrifices. ²He asked them, "Do you think that because these Galileans suffered in this way they were worse sinners than all other Galileans? ³No, I tell you; but unless you repent, you will all perish as they did. ⁴Or those eighteen who were killed when the tower of Siloam fell on them—do you think that they were worse offenders than all the others living in Jerusalem? ⁵No, I tell you; but unless you repent, you will all perish just as they did." ⁶Then he told this parable: "A man had a fig tree planted in his vineyard; and he came looking for fruit on it and found none. ⁷So he said to the gardener, 'See here! For three years I have come looking for fruit on this fig tree, and still I find none. Cut it down! Why should it be wasting the soil?' ⁸He replied, 'Sir, let it alone for one more year, until I dig around it and put manure on it. ⁹If it bears fruit next year, well and good; but if not, you can cut it down.'"

I.   A telling Lenten lesson from caterpillars.

It is easier to stay out than to get out—that is, when it comes to ruts. But given human nature—and our proclivity to exchange one for another—the wiser option of staying out of ruts is not so easy. Maybe the only choice we truly have, given the Fallen state of things, is which rut we will end up in.

Lent summons the faithful to examine their rutted patterns— the unproductive modes of being in the world that keep us from becoming who God calls us to be. An image that illustrates beautifully the nature of our ruttedness comes from the following study done on processionary caterpillars.

It seems that a team of researchers lined up a group of caterpillars around a pot containing a plant which the caterpillars loved to eat. From the lead caterpillar to the last one, they all were lined up in a row—head to head. The lead caterpillar started to move, and then the rest followed. Around and around the rim of the pot they went—for a full week.

Hungry, tired, with their very lives at risk, the caterpillars kept on going. They processed and processed. Not once did they glance over at the plant that could have fed them. Not one of them broke ranks with the others to get off the "merry-go-round" and find relief. Eventually, locked in their pattern of processing, they marched around the rim until they all died.

One way to approach the purpose of Lent—at least early Lent— is to understand it as the Church's way of getting the faithful "unrutted." The call to self-examination, the summons to reflection and renewal, the insistence on "giving something up and taking something on" presume *the need to change.* To become unstuck. To break free. To become, by the grace of God, a free and fruitful child of the Most High.

II. The real roots of ruttedness.

Ruts have always been around, and each of us has his or her favorites. But the ones most commonly mentioned today have their origin in self-concern. Negative body image. Low self-esteem. Procrastination. Perfectionism. Co-dependence. Under-employment. Over-commitment. Too much sugar. Too little sex. Not enough sleep. Credit card balance too high. Not enough free time. A job that isn't satisfying. An addiction hard to break. A marriage that isn't happy. A relationship going nowhere. A lack of friends.

The Church, on the other hand—while not discounting these modern ruts—has maintained that the wider and deeper ruts that keep humanity stuck have their genesis in something more theological than cultural: namely, "the world, the flesh, and the devil," and/or "the seven deadly sins." Compared with these "theological Pharaohs of human bondage," the "ruts" of today are mere flea bites. And the Church has said that our relationship to these perennial, more cosmic ruts needs to be addressed first. Otherwise, Lenten change will mean little more than moving "from rut to rut" in a life of perfect stuckness—and perfect insignificance.

So, how do we get out of being stuck in "the world, the flesh, and the devil"? How do we stay free of the seven deadly ruts— Pride, Greed, Lust, Gluttony, Envy, Anger, and Sloth? How do we escape excessive self-concern that leads to contempt for others? How do we let go of immoderate desire for possessions in general, and the possessions of others in particular? How do we get away from inordinate and misdirected sexual desire? How do we break free from excessive desire for food and drink, and making a god of the belly? How do we let go of the consuming desire for others to be as unsuccessful as we are? How do we free ourselves of pathological anger that destroys both the giver and the recipient? Lastly, how do we break free of torpor, or spiritual apathy?

After considering these major league ruts, most of us would just as soon stick with lowering fat grams or giving up dessert for Lent. But if we want to be more than a barren fig tree, if we want to break free of the "Egypt" of sin and progress toward the "Promised Land" that the Gospel confers, we need to own two things.

III. The "way of the kitten," the "way of the monkey," and Reinhold Niebuhr.

In India, Joseph Campbell found that two rather amusing images were used to portray spiritual growth. One was the "way of the kitten," and the other was the "way of the monkey." When a kitten cries "meow" its mother comes and takes it by the scruff of the neck and carries it away to safety. On the other hand, as anyone who has traveled in India would know, when a band of monkeys comes scampering out of a tree and hits the ground running, the babies riding on their mothers' backs hang on for dear life. They do it by themselves.

Accordingly, Campbell said that the two ways parallel the essence of spiritual growth. Each needs to be balanced with the other. The "way of the kitten" represents the person who prays for the Lord's help—for "outside" help, such as strength, guidance, and an open and loving will. In this "power from outside," the belief "I can't, but God can" is essential. Surrender forms the essence of this prayer for Divine deliverance in the face of human powerlessness—whether it describes the Hebrews in Egypt or someone struggling with an addiction in America.

The "way of the monkey," on the other hand, concerns claiming one's own "power from within." It is the belief that God gave us a mind and a will; that, in many respects, we are not helpless to help ourselves. Like the monkeys, we can "hold on" without outside assistance. We can do whatever God puts within our power to do.

Reinhold Niebuhr's majestic prayer summarizes both the "way of the kitten" and the "way of the monkey." As we seek to get out of the spiritual or physical ruts that bedevil us, both ways need to be employed.

In its full form, this "serenity prayer" goes as follows:

> God, grant me the serenity
> to accept the things I cannot change,
> the courage to change the things I can,
> and the wisdom to know the difference.
>
> Living one day at a time;
> enjoying one moment at a time,
> accepting hardship as the way to peace.
> Taking as He did, this sinful world as it is,
> not as I would have it;
> trusting that He will make all things right
> if I surrender to His will;

that I may be reasonably happy in this life,
and supremely happy with Him forever in the next.
Amen.

10. The Stone That Rules

Luke 20:9-19

⁹Jesus began to tell the people this parable: "A man planted a vineyard, and leased it to tenants, and went to another country for a long time. ¹⁰When the season came, he sent a slave to the tenants in order that they might give him his share of the produce of the vineyard; but the tenants beat him and sent him away empty-handed. ¹¹Next he sent another slave; that one also they beat and insulted and sent away empty-handed. ¹²And he sent still a third; this one also they wounded and threw out. ¹³Then the owner of the vineyard said, 'What shall I do? I will send my beloved son; perhaps they will respect him.' ¹⁴But when the tenants saw him, they discussed it among themselves and said, 'This is the heir; let us kill him so that the inheritance may be ours.' ¹⁵So they threw him out of the vineyard and killed him. What then will the owner of the vineyard do to them? ¹⁶He will come and destroy those tenants and give the vineyard to others." When they heard this, they said, "Heaven forbid!" ¹⁷But he looked at them and said, "What then does this text mean: 'The stone that the builders rejected has become the cornerstone?' ¹⁸Everyone who falls on that stone will be broken to pieces; and it will crush anyone on whom it falls." ¹⁹When the scribes and chief priests realized that he had told this parable against them, they wanted to lay hands on him at that very hour, but they feared the people.

I.   The picture book and the mirror.

Helmut Thielicke, the renowned German scholar/preacher often referred to the parables of Jesus as "God's picture book." Last week, God's picture album closed on a high note indeed. The service ended with the "community of prodigals" having heard, one more time, that "Golden Oldie" of the faithful: "amazing grace" depicted in the Parable of the Prodigal Son.

No wonder the Church calls the Fourth Sunday in Lent "Refreshment Sunday." In the lean Lenten season, this was a "fat" Sunday indeed. We went to our cars high on the merrymaking. We exited full on the fatted calf. We retired reconfirmed in the warmth of grace. We went home heartened by the robe and the ring placed on the wayward lad by his unconditionally loving father. We felt somewhere deep inside that if there was a home for the "prodigal," then there certainly was a "home" out there for us, too. The only "blemish" in the old photo still remained— "Pecksniffe," the sullen older brother, remained outside the party, chafing at his sibling's undeserved good fortune.

Thielicke would also say that taking in the parables of Jesus was a little like seeing his young son sit down for the first time in front of a full-length mirror. At first, the toddler appeared confused by the image he saw. Not recognizing himself, he stared blankly at the mirror. Then, all of a sudden, the expression on his face changed. He began to recognize the similarity between his movements and the corresponding image in the mirror. In an instant, he blurted out proudly: "That's me!"

Thielicke said that the parables of Jesus are often like that for us. We hear the stories as interesting tales, but largely "churchy" ones—ones that never get much past a stunted, stained-glass relevance to the "real world." That is, until, like the toddler, we reach a level of awareness. When the scales fall from our eyes, not only do we "see" the parable, but we see ourselves in it. We say, "That's me!" Depending on where we are in life, we are the "prodigal" coming home from a "far country." We are the elder brother who can't stand for God to do so much for others, and not enough for us. We are the suffering parent who suffers with a child through his or her mistakes.

II. The party is over.

But then the party ends. And with the parable's ending, the Lectionary puts Luke on "fast forward" until we join Jesus teaching in the temple, a few days following the "Triumphal Entry." This parable that Jesus tells does not concern a "merry sinner" like the prodigal. This story is not about a rebellious adolescent who falls prey to "the sins of the flesh," but then comes to his senses. This parable doesn't end with everything turning out pretty much hunky-dory. This story is not about "Brad Pitt" coming home, but about a darker, more sinister reality. A reality that disinclines us to look in the mirror and exclaim: "That's me!"

With an expert writer's keen eye, Annie Dillard treats the chapter on "Luke" in *Incarnation: Contemporary Writers on the New Testament,* edited by Alfred Corn (New York: Viking, 1990). She notes the gathering shift in Luke's narrative and that Jesus' ministry "enlarges in awfulness," from the sunny Galilean days of eating and drinking, teaching and healing by the lakeside (where all is possible through God's power and love)—to a dark messianic journey which begins as soon as Peter acknowledges Jesus as the Christ (9:18-27). On the long journey to Jerusalem, the austerity of Jesus deepens. Dillard says that his "mystery and separateness magnify." He understands more and more that the party is over. The "elder brother" in the prodigal story not only has stayed away from the homecoming; he is violently opposed to it, and will not stand for it anymore.

Dillard says that Jesus " ... does walk, that day, and the next day, and the day following, soberly, wittingly, and freely going up to Jerusalem for the Passover in which he will not be passed over. There is little mingling with the crowds, and only four healings. ... His words are often harsh and angry. 'Thou fool' he has God say to the rich man. 'Ye hypocrites,' he calls his disciples. 'Depart from me all ye workers of iniquity,' the outraged master says. 'Whosoever shall fall upon that stone shall be broken, but on whomsoever it shall fall, it will grind him to powder'" (pp. 33-34).

III. Not retaliation but Resurrection.

"That's me!" we could all say of the "wicked tenants" in the parable for today—notwithstanding the resistance to claiming our own corruption. Maybe we haven't literally mugged a rent collector, or murdered the owner's son, or engineered a "hostile takeover." But, according to Jesus' righteousness of the heart (Mt. 5:21-48), we, like the vineyard terrorists, "have followed too much the devices and desires of our own hearts, we have offended against thy holy laws, we have left undone those things which we ought to have done, and we have done those things which we ought not to have done" *(Book of Common Prayer,* pp. 41-42). A strong chain, we should realize, does not make a vicious dog "good."

So what is the good news? The future—Jesus' future, our future—is in the hands of God. Trust. Despite all appearances to the contrary, God reigns. Do not recall the former things, or "consider the things of old," for God is bringing forth "a new thing" out of the desert (Is. 43:19). Those who sowed with tears will reap "with shouts of joy" (Ps. 126:6). As we forget "what lies behind and [strain] forward to what lies ahead," the "prize" awaits those whom Jesus has made his own (Phil. 3:12-14). And, yes, "the stone that the builders rejected" will become the cornerstone (Lk. 20:17).

How can we be so sure that God "reigns," especially when so much of life invites us to be "of little faith"? The best answer is: *Come and see. Come and experience. Drink deeply into the Paschal mystery revealed most powerfully in the weeks ahead.* Don't allow anything to get in the way. Make a commitment to be there for the Holy Week liturgies. To ride into Jerusalem with Jesus. To having your feet washed. To going through the Stations of the Cross. To arrive, by Holy Saturday, with a feeling of "That's me!" in the Parable of the Wicked Tenants. I *was* there when they crucified my Lord. But don't stop there. Be ready to receive through the Paschal Event a new, emancipated faith-consciousness. Then you will be reminded that God has changed the ending to the Parable of the Wicked Tenants. "What then will the owner of the vineyard do to them? [They say] He will come and destroy those tenants and give the vineyard to others" (vv. 15-16). But "they" get it wrong. The "vineyard owner" does not come to destroy, but to resurrect; he does not show up to retaliate, but to redeem.

We are set free through knowing that if Easter were about retribution, the world would have been vaporized on the "third day"— not saved. Let us never forget, no matter how far down the scale into doubt and despair we have gone, that *the Cornerstone reigns.* Let us be of good cheer.

3-OEHM

11. Jesus and the "Life Review"

Mark (14:32-72) 15:1-39 (40-47)

[1]As soon as it was morning, the chief priests held a consultation with the elders and scribes and the whole council. They bound Jesus, led him away, and handed him over to Pilate. [2]Pilate asked him, "Are you the King of the Jews?" He answered him, "You say so." [3]Then the chief priests accused him of many things. [4]Pilate asked him again, "Have you no answer? See how many charges they bring against you." [5]But Jesus made no further reply, so that Pilate was amazed. [6]Now at the festival he used to release a prisoner for them, anyone for whom they asked. [7]Now a man called Barabbas was in prison with the rebels who had committed murder during the insurrection. [8]So the crowd came and began to ask Pilate to do for them according to his custom. [9]Then he answered them, "Do you want me to release for you the King of the Jews?" [10]For he realized that it was out of jealousy that the chief priests had handed him over. [11]But the chief priests stirred up the crowd to have him release Barabbas for them instead. [12]Pilate spoke to them again, "Then what do you wish me to do with the man you call the King of the Jews?" [13]They shouted back, "Crucify him!" [14]Pilate asked them, "Why, what evil has he done?" But they shouted all the more, "Crucify him!" [15]So Pilate, wishing to satisfy the crowd, released Barabbas for them; and after flogging Jesus, he handed him over to be crucified. ...

I.   Scenes from a life.

The experts on death and dying, such as Elizabeth Kubler-Ross, say that the dying often undergo what is called a "life review" close to the moment of death. Something of a panorama of the life they have lived mysteriously passes before them, and they "review" their personal histories in light of the fast-approaching end.

Each of the four Gospels describes the last moments of Jesus' life in distinctive ways. In Luke, Jesus says, "Father, into your hands I commend my spirit" (23:46). Matthew records, "Jesus cried again in a loud voice and breathed his last" (27:50). In John, Jesus declares, "It is finished" (19:30). And in Mark, the earliest and least adorned of the four, the text says simply: "Jesus gave a loud cry and breathed his last" (15:37). Despite the variance, what all the Evangelists agree on is that Jesus died.

Did Jesus undergo a "life review"? Who can say? Certainly none is ever mentioned in the Gospels. Yet, as you think of him hanging there on Golgotha's tree for hours—like something out of a slaughterhouse—you wonder if the events of Jesus' short life didn't pass before him.

What would he have seen? Would it have begun with his unauthorized stay in Jerusalem, where, as a precocious adolescent, he listened for hours to the teachers, wowing them with his understanding? Or with seeing the traumatized look on his enraged parents' faces—and then recalling how he overrode their protests by having the audacity to ask them where else *should* he be but in his "Father's house" (Lk. 2:41-51)?

Would he have looked back upon his baptism by his fiery cousin, John—and have felt himself going under the chilly Jordan and coming up breathless into the brilliance of the opened heavens, receiving the descent of the Spirit Dove, and hearing the Voice of all voices proclaim the truth that was to be at once his greatest joy and his cross to bear: "You are my Son, the Beloved; with you I am well pleased" (Lk. 3:22)?

Would he have returned to the wilderness temptations, to the weakness of his prolonged fast, and wondered if the temptation to come down off the cross did not exceed by miles the thought of turning rocks into bread, or safely doing somersaults from the spire of the temple?

Would he have remembered his initial return to Nazareth, and how, as a local boy made good, he took the scroll and read from Isaiah's Jubilee—and then had the temerity to say that Isaiah's prophecy had been fulfilled in his very own presence? Would he have recalled how, after then chastising the congregation for hardness of heart, he saw the hometown faithful become a lynch mob, making Jesus forever a fugitive of status quo religion?

Would he have recalled the early morning hours in which Simon Peter came to fetch him so that he could come back to the city limits of Capernaum, and continue what could become a thriving medical practice under the shingle: "Jesus of Nazareth, M. D."? Could he forget the disappointed look on Peter's face—or on the faces of the unhealed in Capernaum—as he made them leave to preach the Gospel elsewhere (Mk. 1:38)?

Would he have recalled the stop-at-no-cost faith that devised the wildly importunate plan to lower a paralyzed friend down through a punched hole in a ceiling? And would he have recalled the exultant look on the man's face when he—to the chagrin of all onlookers—leapt up from his crippling paralysis of guilt after the Son of Man forgave him his sins (Mk. 2:1-12)?

Would Jesus have recalled the exhilaration he felt when the Seventy returned victorious, confirming that the Kingdom's power over evil could be delegated to others? Would he have remembered how his own "cup runneth over" with praise to God in seeing Satan fall like lightning; and his giving thanks that God revealed the saving truth of the Gospel to such "infants" as his disciples (Lk. 10:17-22)?

Would he have looked back on those "glory days" in Galilee, where, as a teacher of unparalleled authority, he taught through parables and aphorisms about the invisible "domain of God"? How all creation is surrounded by another level of reality—brimming with holiness and power—and how this realm could be entered into through the simple trust of a child, and through child-like persistence in asking for it (Mt. 7:7-11)?

Would he have recalled that momentous time at Caesarea

Philippi, when Peter disclosed the mystery of the Incarnation—that Jesus was the Christ—only to turn around, and in the next instant serve as an instrument of Satan in rebuking Jesus for having such morbid ideas as going to Jerusalem to suffer and die (Mk. 8:28-33)?

Would he have remembered the mountaintop ecstasy of the Transfiguration—the holy communion with Moses and Elijah—and then Peter's miss-the-mark insistence that they memorialize the event, a revelation which, in all honesty, could only be preserved in memory, never in man-made booths (Mk. 9:2-8)?

Would he have called to mind his undying love for Jerusalem, the city of God? How he had repeatedly tried to gather the children of the city to him—as a hen gathers her brood under her wings—only to be refused (Lk. 13:34)? And how, on his final "triumphant" visit within her walls, how much he had wished that this time it could have been different—how the "hosannas to the king" were somehow accurate and not off the mark?

Would he have gone over the anguish of how his closest followers flaked out on him in Gethsemane—after he had washed their feet and fed them the Holy Supper of his own broken body and shed blood? Would he remember the kiss? Remember the soldiers armed to the teeth coming to arrest him like a POW, the weaponless "prince of peace"?

II. The message of Palm Sunday: trust.

At its heart, the Passion Sunday drama bespeaks *the power of faithfulness*. Of being true. Of staying the course. Of holding firm—when all that is within you wants to run. When all that is in you wants to abdicate, and to give in to the easier, softer way. But that is not the way of God. Jesus drinks the cup of sacrifice to the dregs—wanting all along for "this cup to pass." Jesus trusts, and trusts to his death.

So should we. In one of the most poignant illustrations I know of, Frederick Buechner speaks of this trust from the anguish of his own life: "I remember sitting parked by the roadside once, terribly depressed and afraid about my daughter's illness and what was going on in our family, when out of nowhere a car came along down the highway with a license plate that bore on it the one word out of all the words in the dictionary that I needed most to see exactly then. The word was TRUST... The owner of the car turned out to be, as I'd suspected, a trust officer in a bank, and not long ago, having read an account I wrote of the incident somewhere, he found out where I lived and one afternoon brought me the license plate itself, which sits propped up on a bookshelf in my house to this day. It is rusty around the edges and a little battered, and it is also as holy a relic as I have ever seen" (from *Listening to Your Life: Daily Meditations with Frederick Buechner,* compiled by George Connor, HarperSanFrancisco, 1992, pp. 326-327.

12. The "Empty Tomb" Is Not Enough

Mark 16:1-8

¹When the sabbath was over, Mary Magdalene, and Mary the mother of James, and Salome bought spices, so that they might go and anoint him. ²And very early on the first day of the week, when the sun had risen, they went to the tomb. ³They had been saying to one another, "Who will roll away the stone for us from the entrance to the tomb?" ⁴When they looked up, they saw that the stone, which was very large, had already been rolled back. ⁵As they entered the tomb, they saw a young man, dressed in a white robe, sitting on the right side; and they were alarmed. ⁶But he said to them, "Do not be alarmed; you are looking for Jesus of Nazareth, who was crucified. He has been raised; he is not here. Look, there is the place they laid him. ⁷But go, tell his disciples and Peter that he is going ahead of you to Galilee; there you will see him, just as he told you." ⁸So they went out and fled from the tomb, for terror and amazement had seized them; and they said nothing to anyone, for they were afraid.

I.   Easter begins with unfolded deck chairs.

Maybe the best place to start an Easter sermon is by citing that theologian extraordinaire, Charles Schulz, in his inimitable "Peanuts." Here goes. Lucy comes up to Charlie Brown and says, "You know, life is like an ocean liner. Some people take their deck chair and put it on the stern, to see where they have been. And some people put their deck chair on the bow, to see where they are going. Charlie Brown, tell me. Where do you want to put your deck chair?" Perplexed momentarily, Charlie Brown looks at Lucy and says, "I don't know. I can't even unfold my deck chair."

The next best place to start is by taking Herbert O'Driscoll's warning to heart. He contends that there is a danger in Easter, and that danger is that we come to church already knowing the outcome of the Paschal drama: *Jesus rose again*. Knowing what is going to be said and sung, we are hardly shocked by this unimaginable, unprecedented event. It is just another one of those feel-good "happy endings." We no longer are drop-jawed—the hair on the back of our necks doesn't stand up—because familiarity has bred, not contempt, but a "ho-hum, of-course-he-rose-on-the-third-day" attitude. The Cross, in this familiar thinking, is hardly a scandal, but a short pause on the entrance ramp to the Victory Superhighway—a highway lined with bunnies and baskets, colored eggs and country club buffets.

But, as Hans Kung has written: "Easter is rightly understood only if the burden and strain of Good Friday are not forgotten." The burden and the strain disclose several things that should never be glossed over, lest Easter lose its goose-bump producing, too-good-to-be-true character.

First, there were no heroes among the followers of Jesus after his arrest. Each and every disciple—not just Judas or Peter—had abandoned Jesus at his hour of greatest need. Only a few women, looking from a distance, were present at his execution. The Cross had sifted his closest followers like wheat. They couldn't even unfold their deck chairs—or hope to.

Second, with the crucifixion and death of Jesus, what we must remember is that all was lost. Jesus and his cause had ended. Everything that he had proclaimed and stood for had been utterly and completely refuted on the cross. Roman law and Jewish piety, the two most noble pillars of culture in the ancient world, had silenced him for good. Law and order had triumphed. The dangerous "seducer of the people," the "blasphemer" and "dangerous heretic," had died a helpless, godless death. Without a doubt,

Jesus and his cause had been defeated. He had been shown to be
another in a long line of deluded "messianic pretenders," who right-
fully earned a humiliating, shaming, and discrediting death.

So when the women who had seen him "crucified, dead, and
buried" went to the tomb to anoint his body with spices, the last
thing they were expecting was "resurrection"—or, for that matter,
an empty tomb containing a young man dressed in a white robe
(Mk. 16:5). They came in a fearful silence punctuated by a con-
cern over who was going to roll away the large stone from the
entrance to the tomb (v. 4). No wonder "terror and amazement"
seized them, and they fled from the tomb.

But the "empty tomb" was not enough—and it never has been.
Was the body of Jesus stolen? Was there confusion about the true
burial place? Had they gone to the wrong grave? Or did the dis-
ciples make the whole thing up—an extreme form of delusional
thinking to compensate for their hellish guilt and grief? Maybe all
these reasons and more are why the "empty tomb" has never been
made a "proof" or an "article" of the Easter faith. We are never
asked to believe *on* it, or *in* it. Perhaps also that is why Paul no-
where mentions the "empty tomb" to support his preaching of the
Risen Christ, and the earliest Christian communities never appeal
to it as a way to convince nonbelievers. All the empty tomb really
says is that "he is not here" (v. 6).

II. "Where, O death, is your sting?"

What the women disclose to us is that *in facing death, if we
look for Jesus, we find the Resurrection.* We cannot force Easter. But
we can come to the tomb. We can come, as those first women
came that morning—in the death of our expectations, in the death
of our self-devised hopes—and show up in our emptiness. Even if
we show up looking only for "what is," we will nevertheless leave
transformed by "what God has done." Come and see that what the
world murders, God resurrects. What the world puts to death,
God raises to life. That God's love has triumphed. That God in

Christ gives us not what we deserve, but vastly more. That we, like the disciples who vacillated in commitment to Jesus, are shown by Easter that Jesus remains wholly committed to us. In spite of. Grace, indeed, is made perfect in weakness (2 Cor. 12:9).

Easter begins with an encounter with the living Christ himself. Resurrection faith started as an experience—an encounter between unbelieving, broken followers, who, by finding Jesus in a wholly new, incorruptible body, were themselves resurrected. It did not start as theological dogma—something that needed to be believed because a Christian told you to. It did not make it as a philosophical principle—a notion that eternal life comes to a corpse as a new mode of existence on par with a butterfly emerging from its cocoon. Easter is coming face to face with a Jesus who has not just reversed death, but has triumphed over it.

The Christian faith unabashedly proclaims this fabulous news. Death, the final enemy, is defeated. "Death has been swallowed up in victory. Where, O death, is your victory? Where, O death, is your sting?" (1 Cor. 15:54-55).

A story is told about the late Episcopal Bishop Warren Chandler that makes just this point. The old bishop lay dying at home in bed. A life-long friend who was sitting by his bedside, holding the bishop's hand, leaned over and asked him how he felt: "Tell me honestly, Warren, do you worry about crossing the river of death?" Bishop Chandler turned his head and replied, "Why? My Father in heaven owns the land on both sides of the river. Why should I be afraid?"

13. Keys to Being

Luke 24:36b-48

36b While the disciples were talking, Jesus himself stood among them and said to them, "Peace be with you." 37 They were startled and terrified, and thought that they were seeing a ghost. 38 He said to them, "Why are you frightened, and why do doubts arise in your hearts? 39 Look at my hands and my feet; see that it is I myself. Touch me and see; for a ghost does not have flesh and bones as you see that I have." 40 And when he had said this, he showed them his hands and his feet. 41 While in their joy they were disbelieving and still wondering, he said to them, "Have you anything here to eat?" 42 They gave him a piece of broiled fish, 43 and he took it and ate in their presence. 44 Then he said to them, "These are my words that I spoke to you while I was still with you— that everything written about me in the law of Moses, the prophets, and the psalms must be fulfilled." 45 Then he opened their minds to understand the scriptures, 46 and he said to them, "Thus it is written, that the Messiah is to suffer and to rise from the dead on the third day, 47 and that repentance and forgiveness of sins is to be proclaimed in his name to all nations, beginning from Jerusalem. 48 And you are witnesses of these things."

I.   "The glory of God is a human being fully alive" —St. Irenaeus (c. 130—c. 200).

The heart of the Easter faith is that those who encountered the Risen Jesus had their lives changed forever. Mind you, the change in character was not a complete, once-and-for-all kind of thing. Like any personal change, it had its ups and downs. But the change that the Resurrection brought into their lives was as unquestionable as it was life-altering. Once-devastated, debilitated followers of Jesus emerged as *new people* unafraid to proclaim the Resurrection everywhere they went—regardless of personal cost. Unfettered by the stigma of the Cross, they boldly announced not only the Gospel of Jesus, but Jesus as the fulfillment of the Gospel. How did they make such a change? What had to happen in their lives to make it so? What needs to happen in our lives to make it so for us?

II. Five ways to be alive.

In a marvelous little book *entitled Fully Human, Fully Alive: A New Life Through a New Vision* (Niles, Ill.: Argus Communications, 1976), John Powell, S. J., outlines five essential components of what he terms "fullness of life." In these keys to abundant living that Fr. Powell discloses, echoes of what happened to change defeated disciples into Easter Christians also become apparent—and worth preaching on during the Great Fifty Days.

A. Accept yourself. Powell maintains that people who are "fully alive" have more than a superficial sense of being loved unconditionally—in spite of their own weakness or corruption. They own their imperfection, because, still deeper, they derive their personal worth from God, not from what they do or don't do. Yet, when they do something well, they don't mind patting themselves on the back. These "self-acceptors" are gentle with themselves. They forgive themselves. Each time they fall down and get back up, they seem to do so without the crippling side-effects of self-loathing or self-condemnation.

Without a doubt, when the Risen Jesus comes into the community of disciples as a "peace bearer" and not a "shame bearer," the first thing that the disciples pick up off the floor is *themselves.* By the grace of Jesus, they no longer consider themselves lower than a speedbump. God in Christ resurrects them out of their self-

rejection, and loves them into accepting themselves—*in spite of.*
And this self-acceptance, coming only out of Jesus-acceptance, forms
the foundation of their Gospel witness.

B. Be yourself. One of the characteristics of the "dried-up life,"
as distinct from the "abundant life," is the attempt to sing some-
body else's song instead of your own. Perhaps out of the fear of
failure or the rejection of others, you live somebody else's life. You
try to be somebody you aren't, and not only get stuck in this rut—
you build a four-bedroom house there and live in it.

Freed by the self-acceptance the Resurrection brought to them,
the disciples could pick themselves up and *follow God's creative call
on their lives.* They could emerge from their safe-deposit existence
to sing a new, unique song called "apostleship." They could be
who God wanted them to be—that is, authoritative witnesses to
the world that the Crucified lives: "This Jesus God raised up, and
of that all of us are witnesses" (Acts 2:32). Or, in the words from
the Epistle of 1 John for today, they could sing: "We declare to
you what was from the beginning, what we have heard, what we
have seen with our eyes, what we have looked at and touched with
our hands, concerning the word of life" (1:1).

C. Forget yourself in loving. Progressing in self-acceptance,
and in the capacity to risk being their true selves, the community
of post-Resurrection believers became *artists at love.* That is, just as
an artist "loses" herself or himself in the creation of a painting or a
sonnet, so too did the primitive community come to "lose them-
selves" in caring for others. They didn't hold back, preoccupied
with their own agenda—worrying about how much of their "pre-
cious time" they could budget to this project or that cause. They
didn't hesitate to expend themselves for one another with a kind of
reckless abandon. They did so not as "do-gooders" looking to have
their charity cards punched, or as "together" people seeking to
assist the "less fortunate"—but as people who had fallen under the
"Godspell" of Jesus and who wanted to love others as freely as

Jesus loved them. No wonder, in the Acts of the Apostles, it was said of the Christians: "All who believed were together and had all things in common; they would sell their possessions and goods and distribute the proceeds to all, as any had need" (2:44-45).

D. Believe. The Resurrection called the disciples to be abundant-livers in another way. It provided them with a specific purpose for their lives, a vocation. What was this calling? To spread the glorious news of what God had done in Christ Jesus, and to show forth what the Resurrection meant for the whole cosmos—the "new exodus" from the "pharaoh" of sin and death. This single-minded commitment to the Easter truth made the overcoming of unimaginable hardship possible for primitive Christianity (cf. 2 Cor. 11:24-28). As Nietzsche would say centuries later: "Anyone who has a 'why,' can endure almost any 'how.'" This deep sense of mission—and the commitment it required—lifted the disciples from the pettiness and aimlessness that can befall the uncommitted, while it also kept them going when the dark night of doubt threatened.

E. Belong. The fifth and final component of the "full life" is to have a sense of community. To belong to a "family" in which people are "for" one another, and you are missed if you aren't present. This means a community where you can be accepted, supported, challenged—as well as corrected. A community that calls you to accountability for your gifts, but in a way that "builds up" rather than "tearing down." A community that is open and clear about its values, yet also flexible in dealing with the life circumstances that make for exceptions to the rule. Most of all, we need a community that is constant, that does not flee when times get tough, or when bad things happen.

The community of the Resurrection became just such a community for Gospel believers. Without such a community, the New Creation would hardly have gotten off the ground. And the Jesus Movement would have vanished, lost forever in the dustbins of history.

14. Shepherd of Us All

John 10:22-30

22At that time the festival of the Dedication took place in Jerusalem. It was winter, 23and Jesus was walking in the temple, in the portico of Solomon. 24So the Jews gathered around him and said to him, "How long will you keep us in suspense? If you are the Messiah, tell us plainly." 25Jesus answered, "I have told you, and you do not believe. The works that I do in my Father's name testify to me; 26but you do not believe, because you do not belong to my sheep. 27My sheep hear my voice. I know them, and they follow me. 28I give them eternal life, and they will never perish. No one will snatch them out of my hand. 29What my Father has given me is greater than all else, and no one can snatch it out of the Father's hand. 30The Father and I are one."

I.   The community of the Resurrection.

The presence of the Christian community constitutes the greatest "proof" of Easter. Let's face it. After the crucifixion, there was no "viable" community centered around the man Jesus—only a handful of worrywarts. In a very real sense, the disciples had been "crucified, made dead, and buried" along with Jesus on that terrible Friday. Until Sunday, they too had descended into "hell."

That is why the whole Christian faith stands or falls on Easter—not the Cross. New life, not suffering and death, occupy the heart of the faith. The Suffering Servant easters into the Risen Lord, and assures us that God's final word is not tragedy, but victory. As Paul put it: "If Christ has not been raised, your faith is futile and you are still in your sins. ... [We] are of all people most to be pitied" (1 Cor. 15:17-19). Otherwise, Easter becomes merely another Hallmark moment, a day for bunnies, baskets, and blossoms—all set around an hour of loud, majestic music.

The gathered Christian community is, therefore, the "sacrament" of Easter. It is the "outward and visible sign" that God's love has triumphed. Walking, talking, and eating with the Risen Christ—who is not just a phantom—they are "resurrected" by Christpower. They come forward from the Resurrection wholly different people. Whereas before they cowered, now they are committed. Before they fled with only the thought of saving their own skins; now they become reckless and bold—sparing no efforts even in the face of death—to proclaim Jesus as the Christ. No psychology, no "group theory," no "sociology of religion" can explain such a spontaneous reversal in the disciples of Jesus after their trauma. Only the mystery of Resurrection can suffice.

II. The continuing community.

But how was the community of Jesus to continue to live together after the Easter "honeymoon" had ended? After Jesus had departed from them, and their feet hit the ground, then what? What was to characterize their fellowship? What kind of community were they to be? How could they continue to be these Easter people, day after day? Those are some of the questions that this "Good Shepherd" Sunday seeks to answer.

Herbert O'Driscoll maintains that the Gospel reading for today gives us the answers we need in providing a "portrait" of the Easter people, in their ongoing life as "undershepherds" to the Good Shepherd. They are well worth considering—and holding up to the current state of our own Christian communities.

A. The community is where the voice of the Good Shepherd is "heard" (v. 27). An intentional "listening for the voice" of the Risen Christ, through the working of the Holy Spirit, underpins the whole spectrum of Christian living. In personal and corporate prayer, we listen for the voice. In the reading of Scripture, we listen for the voice. In worship and in the sacraments, we listen for the voice. In the sharing of our lives with one another, we listen for the voice. In responding to the needs of others placed before us, we listen for the voice.

Developing "attentiveness to God's voice," as Henri Nouwen has said, is fundamental to living the spiritual life—but it is also one of the hardest things to cultivate. For instance, Nouwen compared one of the first stages of listening prayer to a person who, after years of living with open doors, suddenly decides to shut them. Visitors who used to come and enter the home start pounding on the doors, wondering why they are not allowed to enter. Only when they realize that they are no longer welcome do the visitors desist. His point: many distractions occur when we seek to listen to the Good Shepherd's voice. Persist, and they will slowly become less and less distracting.

B. Community is where we have a sense of being "known" (v. 27). Intimacy lies at the heart of the Christian Gospel. Intimacy with God. Intimacy with other believers. Intimacy with oneself. Intimacy, through the Spirit, with "strangers" or even "enemies." The community of the Resurrection, especially as depicted in John's tenth chapter, derives its life from the sacred intimacy it shares with the Good Shepherd—and by extending this intimacy to all.

Is our faith community a safe place in which to be known, or to risk being known *beyond a superficial level?* Is it a place where we can be *accepted* after we are known? Author M. Scott Peck, while in Atlanta doing a workshop on "community," emphasized this kind of vulnerability as a cornerstone of authentic, versus pseudo, community. Then he asked the participants to break into small groups and to risk sharing something of themselves with each other. During a break, a woman came up to him and started telling him about a painful divorce she was going through, and how her children were having a difficult time. Peck interrupted her after a few minutes and asked why she didn't share this with her small group.

She looked at him dumbfounded and said, "You don't understand. I can't tell all this in my group. Three people who go to my church are in there!"

C. Community is where we "follow" Jesus in the faith (v. 27). Listening, opening ourselves up to the Good Shepherd to be intimately known, leads naturally into "followership." The theologian H. A. Williams once said: "The opposite of sin can only be faith, not virtue." Therefore, followership in the community of the Resurrection is marked not by perfection, but by faith *in spite of imperfection.* Goodness, which even Jesus would attribute only to God, is not self-generated in the Christian community, but is derived from being "in Christ." Jesus, the Risen One, becomes the one without whom we cannot live, and *following* is our way of living in Christ. Perhaps that is why Jesus never asked his disciples to *love* him, but to *follow* him.

D. Community is where we experience "eternal life" (v. 28). In the Fourth Gospel, "eternal life" means *sharing in the being of God.* Through intimate followership with the Risen One, the believer experiences "eternal life" or "the being of God." To share in this supernatural reality—this true and abiding Presence—is what transforms a gathering of people into *a faith community.* "Permanent being" suffuses "transient being"; in that suffusion, or mutual indwelling, we experience a sort of "promissory note" or "downpayment" on the fullness of the Holy Eternal which is to come. Thus "eternal life" occurs wherever God meets us, and it cannot be "snatched away." William Temple summed up this truth beautifully when he said, "The life of faith does not earn eternal life; it is eternal life. And Christ is its vehicle."

15. Following a Simple Path

John 14:23-29

²³Jesus said to Judas (not Iscariot), "Those who love me will keep my word, and my Father will love them, and we will come to them and make our home with them. ²⁴Whoever does not love me does not keep my words; and the word that you hear is not mine, but is from the Father who sent me. ²⁵I have said these things to you while I am still with you. ²⁶But the Advocate, the Holy Spirit, whom the Father will send in my name, will teach you everything, and remind you of all that I have said to you. ²⁷Peace I leave with you; my peace I give to you. I do not give to you as the world gives. Do not let your hearts be troubled, and do not let them be afraid. ²⁸You heard me say to you, 'I am going away, and I am coming to you.' If you loved me, you would rejoice that I am going to the Father, because the Father is greater than I. ²⁹And now I have told you this before it occurs, so that when it does occur, you may believe."

I. "The Gospel in soundbites."

Lynn Garrett, religion editor for *Publishers Weekly*, was quoted in the "Life" section of *USA Today* as saying: "Spiritual seekers investigating a wide range of expressions are unlikely to turn to traditional clergy with their religious questions."

So where do these "spiritual seekers" go? They go to bookstores—religious bookstores, so the growing numbers and profits say. And there they look not so much for profound theological or philosophical thought, but for practical advice. "10 Ways to Becoming a Spiritual Person" sells much better than "What Does Being Spiritual Mean?"

This trend is true in part because of the nature of American life, summed up in the phrase: "Time is money." Time management (or time obsession) isn't just for Harvard Business grads any more, but for everybody.

Take, for instance, a study in the mid-1990s of 200 executives conducted by Accountemps, a personnel agency. When the dust settled, Accountemps found that on average executives spent 15 minutes a day on telephone hold, which amounted to 7.5 days per year. They spent 32 minutes a day reading "unnecessary mail," which came to 16 hours per year. "Unnecessary meetings" logged in at 72 minutes per day—or 36 hours per year.

What were the "wasted totals"? Almost 2 hours per day, or about 2 months per year. "Mea maxima culpa!" the executives said, and repented of this "waste" immediately.

No wonder not just executives but all the rest of us have had it drummed into us to hunt for streamlinization everywhere, for speed and efficiencies of every sort and condition. Time is money. The upshot, of course, is that in this world, "personal reflection" is an indulgence the hurried can't afford.

And, like it or not, the consumer world carries this cultural "hurry up" attitude into religion. Something on the order of "spirituality on the go," or "take-home religion," is the order of the day. Call it: "The Gospel in soundbites."

II. The "simple path" of Mother Teresa.

Today's Gospel reading lends itself to a "how to" answer. That is, the Christian community faces a question that has endured for two millennia since: "How can disciples have a personal relationship with Jesus when he has gone?"

John's Jesus provides two answers to the dilemma. The disciple can continue in a close personal relationship with the Risen

Jesus by doing two things: by *doing the works of Jesus* (14:12-14), and *by keeping his commandments* (14:15-24).

What does it mean to do the works of Jesus? Walk on water? Multiply loaves? Change water into wine? Heal lepers and raise the dead? Get crucified? Maybe before trying to run the 100-yard dash with the Messiah, we should start out with some baby steps in "doing the works of Jesus."

Some teachings by Mother Teresa, compiled in a marvelous book by Lucinda Vardey called, *A Simple Path* (New York: Ballantine, 1995), suggest a number of straightforward, yet profound ways that the seeker can begin to have a close personal relationship with the unseen Christ.

Mother Teresa says to *start out your day in silence.* Find some silence every day, somewhere, even if it is just for a few minutes. In the silence, be still. Get quiet. Slow down. What follows might seem awkward and wasteful (since time is money), *but keep at it.* Just as Jesus sought out the silence of the desert to commune with his Abba God, so should we. No, you don't need a Range Rover to do this. Save time and money: simply go into the "desert" of your "room" (or your quiet space). It is in the quietness of the heart that God speaks, Mother Teresa said, and so we must set aside that time for God alone to encounter us. She adds, "God is the friend of silence."

The Father "who sees in secret" will reward you (Mt. 6:6), Jesus said; and the reward will be deepened *prayer* that comes out of the silence. Prayer is to the soul what blood is to the body, Mother Teresa taught. In other words, you cannot begin to do the works of Jesus—or keep his commandments—without prayer. Put simply, there is no Kingdom of God without God. Thus, starting in silence and moving into prayer is like getting a spiritual transfusion every day. Through the Holy Spirit in prayer, the vitality of the New Creation courses through our veins, and we come alive.

Out of silence and prayer emerges *faith.* "Faith" here does not mean believing what you know isn't so. Nor does it imply gullibility—a belief in things for which there is no evidence. Genuine faith never has, never will mean that. As Tillich said, "faith" means "being grasped by a power greater than we are, a power that shakes us and turns us and transforms us and heals us. Surrender to this power is faith." Thus faith is the gift of God, an awareness that builds and grows through prayer. When one takes on this attitude of surrender—this faith—all things are possible for the believer (Mt. 17:20).

Being grasped by faith imbues the believer with the most excellent gift of all: the gift of *love*. "We must be loved by God first," Mother Teresa contended, "and only then can we give to others. ... When you know how much God is in love with you then you can only live your life radiating that love." Does this love mean going to the Third World to serve the poor? Perhaps. But Mother Teresa insisted that this Divine radiance first be directed toward those closest to you: at home, at work, in your own neighborhood and city. She knew how much easier it was to love people "far away" than to love them nearby. Lastly, she said, it isn't so much what we do as it is the quality of love we put into doing it.

Peace through service ends her list. Mother Teresa quotes Gandhi, who said, "Act, but seek not the fruit of your action." Service and peace come together when we let go of "results." The book ends with the following quote titled ANYWAY, taken from a sign on the wall of Shishu Bhavan, the children's home in Calcutta. It sums up this detachment in service that leads to peace:

"People are unreasonable, illogical, and self-centered. LOVE THEM ANYWAY. If you do good, people will accuse you of selfish, ulterior motives. DO GOOD ANYWAY. If you are successful, you win false friends and true enemies. SUCCEED ANYWAY. The good you will do will be forgotten tomorrow. DO GOOD ANYWAY. Honesty and frankness make you vulnerable. BE HONEST AND FRANK ANYWAY. What you spent your years building may be destroyed overnight. BUILD ANYWAY. People really need help but may attack you if you help them. HELP PEOPLE ANYWAY. Give the world the best you have and you'll get kicked in the teeth. GIVE THE WORLD THE BEST YOU'VE GOT ANYWAY." Amen.

16. "Almost Everybody Dies"

Luke 24:49-53

Jesus said to his disciples, [49]"See, I am sending upon you what my Father promised; so stay here in the city until you have been clothed with power from on high." [50]Then he led them out as far as Bethany, and, lifting up his hands, he blessed them. [51]While he was blessing them, he withdrew from them and was carried up into heaven. [52]And they worshiped him, and returned to Jerusalem with great joy; [53]and they were constantly in the temple blessing God.

I.   Death as a prone camel.

If you have ever been to an open-casket funeral, you know that feeling. You look at persons you have experienced as alive, and you can't see them the same way when they are dead. Even the best of mortuary cosmetologists cannot deny the eerie change. Putting the deceased in their favorite clothes and caking their faces with make-up and mascara cannot counteract the macabre feeling. No wonder cremation is gaining in popularity. Who wouldn't rather look at a capped urn filled with dust?

So what do the Feast of the Ascension and open-casket funerals have in common? This. Simply this. *We do not belong to this world.* As a Persian proverb goes: "Death is a camel that lies down at every door." My door. Your door. Everyone's door. No matter how much funeral homes try to deny the reality—death is the one inevitable fact of natural life. We may conquer global warming, or totalitarian rule, or the common cold, but we will never conquer death. The camel will always show up. Ultimately, we do not belong to this world.

Benjamin Franklin said that *taxes,* along with death, make up the two "inevitables" of existence. But "Poor Richard" and his "Almanac" should look again. You don't *have* to pay "Caesar" a red cent. If you don't, "Caesar" will take good care of you. He'll provide you a place to stay, give you three meals a day, offer you time in a library, a TV room, and a place to exercise. All free. And you can enjoy the striped sunshine for an extended stay.

No, death is the only inevitable in life. As Bernie Siegel, M. D., the celebrated author of *Love, Medicine, and Miracles,* has written: "Almost everybody dies." Which means that we all live under a "deadline," like it or not. And it also means that *life is a gift.* We are gifted into this world, we dwell in it for a period of time, and then we leave it. Not necessarily by choice, but we do leave it.

The Ascension of Jesus brings home the point. It declares to us that, like Jesus himself, we belong to God. We are *gifted* into the world, but not *tied* to it. We are spiritual beings first, and worldlings second. Our true home is in heaven. Our enduring place is the realm of the Spirit, not the realm of what we regard as the "real world." We belong to God—not to our spouses. Not to our children. Not to our jobs. Not to our homes and neighborhood. Not to our churches, or to our schools or civic clubs, as wonderful and fulfilling as these things are. We are citizens of heaven, not of earth. Only love in this world has survival value; it never ends (1 Cor. 13:8).

II. Hold everything lightly—especially yourself.

Since our lives are gifts, as is life itself—rather than lamenting the fact, the Ascension tells us to live each day "eschatologically"— that is, *as if it were our last.* To live the way the cancer patients I work with at St. Mark's Episcopal Church in Dalton, Georgia, do. They know more about "daily giftedness" than most of us. They have come to realize, in ways I cannot fathom, that their "deadline" could lie around the corner; and yet each of them has regarded this newfound awareness as making life all the more sacred. The "normal" things of life—friends, family, work, and play—can no longer be taken for granted the way they were before. These patients have come to see them as priceless gifts, given for a time—gifts that will eventually pass away.

Second, the Ascension of Jesus means that we are to *hold lightly the things of this world.* It is like holding a wet sponge so that no water seeps out of it; that is the "grip pressure" on this world the Gospel tells us to have. Hold everything lightly, softly—even tenderly ... as you would cup in your hands a small bird that has fallen out of its nest. Hold your children that way. Your family that way. Your friends that way. Your position in the world that way. The things you have done, or wished to have done, that way. Savor them, delight in them, but hold them gingerly as gifts—not as everlasting entitlements. The people I have seen die the best deaths—though none has gone easily—have practiced this "light-grip pressure" secret to living.

III. The "festival of the future" frees us to be the best we can be.

The noted Roman Catholic theologian, Karl Rahner, said of the departure of Christ from the world to the "right hand of God": "The Ascension is a festival of the future of the world. The flesh is redeemed and glorified, for the Lord is risen forever. We Christians, therefore, are the most sublime of materialists."

The Ascension means that all of historical existence—our day-to-day lives in particular—must be seen from the point of view of the *future.* We look at all that occurs in the world not by human standards, nor by the world's values, but by the future that is in the hands of God. The Ascension declares that *God's full creativity lies ahead of us, not behind us.* God's power and might have not been exhausted in this world, but will reach their consummation in the future. Today, as if putting on a pair of glasses, we look through the lenses of the Ascension; we see the world from Above. We see that all things will find their consummation in God. And we can let go. We don't have to be in control.

The good news of Jesus' exaltation is that cancer is not the final thing. Nor is poverty or depression or alienation or addiction. Neither are earthquakes or tsunamis or meteors headed for earth—just as the horror of the Cross was not the final thing. In the Ascension these things are revealed for what they are: always next-to-the-last things. They do not rule; God does.

If God will ultimately reign, as the Ascension discloses, what are we worldlings to do *now?* Sit back and wait? Become Christian couch potatoes? Hardly. As Mother Teresa said, "We can do no great things; only small things with great love." Martin Luther King, Jr., said the same thing in another way:

"If a man is called to be a street sweeper, he should sweep streets even as Michelangelo painted, or Beethoven composed music. He should sweep streets so well that all the host of heaven and earth will pause and say that here lived a great sweeper who did his job well."

Because we affirm that our final destination lies with the exalted Jesus—with the saints in Light—we live abundantly in this world. We can live freely, lightly manifesting grace with gladness and singleness of heart.

17. God Is a Surprise

John 20:19-23
Acts 2:1-11

¹When the day of Pentecost had come, they were all together in one place. ²And suddenly from heaven there came a sound like the rush of a violent wind, and it filled the entire house where they were sitting. ³Divided tongues, as of fire, appeared among them, and a tongue rested on each of them. ⁴All of them were filled with the Holy Spirit and began to speak in other languages, as the Spirit gave them ability. ⁵Now there were devout Jews from every nation under heaven living in Jerusalem. ⁶And at this sound the crowd gathered and was bewildered, because each one heard them speaking in the native language of each. ⁷Amazed and astonished, they asked, "Are not all these who are speaking Galileans? ⁸And how is it that we hear, each of us, in our own native language? ⁹Parthians, Medes, Elamites, and residents of Mesopotamia, Judea and Cappadocia, Pontus and Asia, ¹⁰Phrygia and Pamphylia, Egypt and the parts of Libya belonging to Cyrene, and visitors from Rome, both Jews and proselytes, ¹¹Cretans and Arabs—in our own languages we hear them speaking about God's deeds of power."

I. Pentecost: Thanksgiving and the Fourth of July rolled into one.

They must have been tired of living out of suitcases for over a month. Tired of writing postcards, or making long-distance calls night after night, instead of seeing their loved ones in person. Tired of adding to their credit-card, Marriott-mired existence for seven weeks. Tired of religion. Tired of eating unfamiliar food, sleeping on an unfamiliar bed, and getting woken up every morning by an unfamiliar phone call from an unfamiliar operator. Even Tom Bodett would have had enough of this.

They must have longed for home, these pilgrims who had come to Jerusalem to celebrate the high holy days. Talk about "motley crews." Parthians, Medes, Elamites, Mesopotamians, Cappadocians, Romans, Egyptians, Cretans, and even Arabs, Luke tells us (Acts 2:9-11). Pluralism plus. Multi-culturalism to the second power. So why were all these Jews from "every nation under heaven" (v. 5) residing in Jerusalem?

"The day of Pentecost had come ... " (Acts 2:1), which meant that the people who had been in Jerusalem for forty-nine days were probably filled with that paradoxical feeling we all get at the end of a long trip—needing to stay, but wanting to go. But long pilgrimages, like long trips, need to end on a significant note, and that high note was the Jewish feast called "Pentecost." "Pentecost" means "fiftieth," which indicated that it fell on the fiftieth day after Passover, marking the ingathering of the first fruits of the harvest. Since it was the second of three obligatory observances devout Jews were to keep (the other two being Passover and Tabernacles), nobody had dared catch an early flight out of Jerusalem that morning.

Later in the Hellenistic Period, Pentecost's association with agriculture began to wane. And in its place, especially after the destruction of the temple in A. D. 70, a new emphasis on Pentecost came about which recognized and celebrated the giving of the Law on Mount Sinai. So there you have it. The Jewish equivalent of Thanksgiving and the Fourth of July rolled into one.

II. The coming of the Second Emmanuel.

Feasting? Yes. Fireworks? Yes. The Risen Jesus returning to his community in "tongues of flame"? Get real. Yet that is what Luke reports. He describes one of the most startling, UFO-like events in the New Testament. When Jesus had told the disciples about the promise of the Father which would clothe them with "power from on high" (Lk. 24:49)—could these disciples have had any inkling of what that promise would mean? Could they have fathomed the sky-high implications it would have for them? I doubt it. I suspect they went to the temple that day to celebrate, with fellow Jews near and far, the Thanksgiving/Fourth of July extravaganza they called Pentecost.

The Dean of the Cathedral of St. John the Divine in New York City, Harry Pritchett, once wrote a song for kids called "Surprise, Surprise, God Is a Surprise." Similarly, behind the Resurrection of Jesus from the dead, the coming of the Holy Ghost in a "violent wind" and in "tongues, as of fire" comes as the second biggest "surprise" in the New Testament. Pentecost—the New Pentecost—falls out of the heavens on the surprised disciples, who immediately begin to communicate in the language of heaven. No interpreters needed here. At long last, Babel is reversed and people actually *hear* each other.

The "Second Jesus," the "Second Emmanuel" bursts upon this unsuspecting gathering of Jesus people. Jesus, in the power of the Spirit, has returned. The wind and flame mark the "Second Incarnation." And the disciples overflow with this intoxicating, Jesus-exalting Presence—so much so that Peter almost gets a DUI on the way home.

III. Three "trademarks" of the Holy Spirit's presence.

In a series of broadcast talks given in Advent of 1935 (later published as *The Spiritual Life)*, the anointed teacher of spirituality, Evelyn Underhill, cited the writings of St. John of the Cross (1542—1591) in terms of the operation of the Holy Spirit in and through believers. The sixteenth-century mystic—who combined the sensitivity of a poet with the intellectual capacity of a trained theologian—said that there were three "trademarks," or "distinguishing characteristics" that the Holy Spirit produced in the heart anchored in God. Underhill expanded on these three things, which are worth noting on Whitsunday:

Tranquillity. A sense of peace accompanies the abiding presence of the Holy Spirit. Call it a "Divine detachment." When a person experiences the Holy Spirit, what Underhill calls the "fuss and feverishness of anxiety, intensity, intolerance, instability, pessimism, and wobble of hurry and worry"—the tell-tale signs of being self-made and self-directed—begin to melt away. The early Christian mystics called this engraced peace *apathaeia* (from which we derive the word "apathy"). It did not mean that the Holy Spirit caused people to become a band of believing blobs—caring less about anything or anybody else but themselves. What it did mean is that the Holy Spirit allowed them to "die to self and neighbor" so that true service, not manipulation, could occur. And the result was a deep sense of personal peace. To forsake judging others, to give up self-justification through achievement and performance, to let go of outcomes according to our preconceived notions—that is what happens in the Tranquillity of the Spirit.

Gentleness. The true test of the spiritual life is how we handle the ups and downs of life. Life's inequalities, emotional or professional disappointments, the sudden intervention of bad fortune—as well as a rising and falling religious temperature—are temptations to self-loathing and self-regret. They are tremendous invitations to deal harshly, and in ugly ways, with ourselves and others. Gentleness is the Spirit's gift of self-acceptance and other-acceptance. It refuses to "solve" problems through violence in all forms. The desire to deal harshly or meanly with anybody or anything gets removed. Gentleness, as a quality of the Holy Spirit's presence in the believer, confirms through an "inner knowing" that Divine love is not limited, that God (somehow) is working through all things, great and small ... that Jesus has indeed "overcome the world."

Strength. This is not spirituality on steroids. It is "steadiness in the Spirit." The capacity to "stick it out." And this kind of strength is a cooperation with God that flows from communion with God. Call it "soul force." It comes from having a keen sense of self-knowledge that leads to "willing one thing," as Kierkegaard maintained. Strength, as Gandhi and Martin Luther King, Jr., demonstrated, did not come from wealth or power, but from "purity of heart." They were able to return love for hate, respect for contempt, and to stand firm against injustice.

Early in Gandhi's life, he was confronted by the head of the Transvaal government in South Africa, General Jan Smuts. Sitting before the imposing Boer soldier, Gandhi informed him quietly, "I've come to tell you that I am going to fight against your government." Smuts smiled incredulously and said, "You mean you have come here to tell me that?" Then he mocked Gandhi: "Is there anything more you want to say?" Unperturbed, Gandhi said, "Yes, there is ... I am going to win." Smuts, astonished, asked Gandhi, "Well, how are you going to do that?" Gandhi smiled and replied, "With your help." Years later Smuts admitted—not happily— that this is exactly what Gandhi did. His "purity of heart," or spiritual strength, led many historians to look upon the twentieth century not as the age of the atom, but as the age of Gandhi.

18. God Above, With, and For Us

John 16:(5-11) 12-15

⁵*Jesus said to them, "Now I am going to him who sent me; yet none of you asks me, 'Where are you going?' ⁶But because I have said these things to you, sorrow has filled your hearts. ⁷Nevertheless I tell you the truth: it is to your advantage that I go away, for if I do not go away, the Advocate will not come to you; but if I go, I will send him to you. ⁸And when he comes, he will prove the world wrong about sin and righteousness and judgment: ⁹about sin, because they do not believe in me; ¹⁰about righteousness, because I am going to the Father and you will see me no longer; ¹¹about judgment, because the ruler of this world has been condemned. ¹²I still have many things to say to you, but you cannot bear them now. ¹³When the Spirit of truth comes, he will guide you into all the truth; for he will not speak on his own, but will speak whatever he hears, and he will declare to you the things that are to come. ¹⁴He will glorify me, because he will take what is mine and declare it to you. ¹⁵All that the Father has is mine. For this reason I said that he will take what is mine and declare it to you."*

I. Yogi Berra, Jay Leno—and a Bible quiz.

"It's deja vu all over again," Yogi Berra would quip, and not necessarily in reference to baseball. It could have been in church as he watched the liturgical wheel turn once again to that Sunday immediately following Whitsunday—Trinity Sunday. "*Holy, Holy, Holy* ... all over again." And with the "deja vu" comes that blank feeling about this deepest, most central, most enigmatic of all Christian mysteries.

The quest is not for the faint of heart, especially given the cyber-filled, soundbite-driven world in which we live. Explanations of the Trinity may well draw yawns—they have for centuries—but now they may also draw blank stares. God in three persons. Say *what?* Christina Hoff Sommers, a professor of philosophy at Clark College, who has written articles on gender bias and moral chaos in education for the *New England Journal of Medicine*, the *Wall St. Journal,* and the *Chicago Tribune*—and who has made appearances on *20/20, Donahue, 60 Minutes,* and *Nightline*—shared the following vignette. It reveals quite a lot about the state of the culture we address on this Trinity Sunday.

On a recent *Tonight Show,* host Jay Leno did one of his "man-on-the-street" interview sessions. This night, the subject was biblical competency. So Leno collared two college-age women and asked them, "Can you name one of the Ten Commandments?" One replied eagerly, "Sure, freedom of speech!" Leno then passed the mike to another twenty-something: "OK, complete this sentence, 'Let the one who is without sin ... '" The man, smiling knowingly, responded, "Have a good time." Baffled, Leno then turned to another young man and asked, "OK, this is an easy one. Who in the Bible was eaten by the whale?" Out came the confident answer, "Pinnochio."

II. The God of their understanding.

The doctrine of the Holy Trinity began first as an experience. The God of the matriarchs and the patriarchs—the Holy One of Israel—was known primarily as "the One who responds." A "personal" God. The One who creates. The One who calls. The One who remains faithful. The One who liberates. The One who gifts the Law. The One who judges and corrects out of love. The One who promises and keeps those promises. A wonderful illustration of this truth comes from the following Hasidic tale:

> When Rabbi Menachem Mendel was a small child, his grandfather, Rabbi Shneur Zalman, held him on his lap and asked the child, "Where is *Zeide* [grandfather]?"
>
> The child touched his grandfather's nose. "No, that is *Zeide's* nose. But where is *Zeide?*"
>
> The child touched the grandfather's beard. "No, that is *Zeide's* beard. But where is *Zeide?*"
>
> The child jumped down out of his grandfather's lap and scurried into the next room where he shouted, "*Zeide!*" Rabbi Zalman got to his feet and went into the next room. Gleefully, the child pointed at him and said, "There is *Zeide!*"

The point: *Zeide* is the one who responds when called. Likewise, we know God through response; God is "the One who responds."

Similarly, the followers of Jesus knew the God of Israel as the Responder. Daily, they would affirm the "credo" of the Hebrew people: "Hear, O Israel: The Lord our God is one Lord" (Dt. 6:4). Israel dwelled under the authority of a strict monotheism. Unlike many other cultures which believed in multiple gods, Israel affirmed belief in One Deity alone. For any other "god" to be put alongside the Holy One was intolerable in all circumstances. The God of Israel called for an exclusive, single-minded allegiance.

Yet, for the disciples of Jesus, the word "God" did not seem to be enough to describe the fullness of their experience. Their encounter with Jesus, and what occurred to them through his death and Resurrection, called for a widened confession with a widened language. Yes, God was One and Sovereign—and wholly Other. Nevertheless, in the person of Jesus they experienced what they came to name as Immanuel: "God with us."

Mind you, this "Immanuel belief" did not take the form of speculating about Jesus' *nature* or *essence,* it simply flowed from what they experienced Jesus *doing*. He acted like God: He raised the dead. He cleansed lepers. He expelled demons with a word. He taught with Divine authority and wisdom. He welcomed fellowship with sinners—actually forgiving them—something God alone had the right to do. Paradoxically, he died the death of a sinner—a refuted heretic and a deluded Messiah. Yet, to their utter surprise, the Father-God whom Jesus proclaimed *raised him from death*. Only then could they speak of Jesus as "Lord" and "Savior," the One who is "far above all rule and authority and power and dominion, and above every name that is named ... " (Eph. 1:21).

III. God over us. God with us and for us. God in and among us.

Jesus was not only anointed by the Holy Spirit at his baptism; he promised this Holy Spirit to his followers after his physical departure. And this personal Spirit-presence comes to the community in the name of Jesus (Jn. 14:26). Furthermore, the Holy Spirit will remain with the followers of Jesus, as he himself had been with them—only in an unseen way (Jn. 14:16). The Holy Spirit will be Jesus among them as their Advocate and Guide. Sound confusing? One-in-three? Three-in-One? One God, yet three names—two of which are male? Is this passé or what?

Cut to the chase. The state of our world demands no less. Trinitarian belief, simply put, comes as a gift to the believing community gathered in Jesus' name. These followers of Jesus looked around to find appropriate language to put words around this experience. In effect, what they came up with was this: *There exists one personal, loving God who functions in three different ways at the same time. God as Creator. God as Savior. God as Life-Giver/Life-Renewer.*

Only God knows God, in the final analysis. But until we see God "face to face," we Christians will have to live with "word-induced ambiguity." We will have to live with the ongoing "creatureliness of words." *God over us. God with us and for us. God in and among us.* Holy, Holy, Holy. If that doesn't fully explain the mystery of the Holy Trinity, take heart. The Bible doesn't explain it either. Furthermore, no Christian is ever asked to believe in a doctrine—only in the living God. Breathe easier still: we are saved by grace, not by our picture-perfect belief. "Believer's righteousness" is not a salvational ATM card that will force God to open the gates of Paradise to us. Thank God! Amen.

19. A Tale of Two Lives

Matthew 10:(16-23) 24-33

Jesus said, ²⁴"A disciple is not above the teacher, nor a slave above the master; ²⁵it is enough for the disciple to be like the teacher, and the slave like the master. If they have called the master of the house Beelzebul, how much more will they malign those of his household! ²⁶So have no fear of them; for nothing is covered up that will not be uncovered, and nothing secret that will not become known. ²⁷What I say to you in the dark, tell in the light; and what you hear whispered, proclaim from the housetops. ²⁸Do not fear those who kill the body but cannot kill the soul; rather fear him who can destroy both soul and body in hell. ²⁹Are not two sparrows sold for a penny? Yet not one of them will fall to the ground apart from your Father. ³⁰And even the hairs of your head are all counted. ³¹So do not be afraid; you are of more value than many sparrows. ³²Everyone therefore who acknowledges me before others, I also will acknowledge before my Father in heaven; ³³but whoever denies me before others, I also will deny before my Father in heaven."

I.   Two men, two futures, two outcomes.

Two men grow up in ways uncannily similar to each other. Both are born into stable, respectable families that dwell in small communities, each near a large metropolis. One grows up in Anathoth, a suburb of Jerusalem, and the other in Lombard, Illinois, a suburb of Chicago.

Their early years seem to be as normal as anyone else's, except, early on, they both show signs of being exceptionally intelligent, and of becoming students of great promise. Their precociousness is confirmed in the large amount of reading they do, and the grades they receive in school. Both seem to have a bright future.

Emotionally, however, being exceptional causes them some problems. Sensitive, they are given to intense inner feelings, which leads to noticeable introspection. They have a hard time making, and keeping, close friends. They have difficulty keeping steady employment, and they have a terrible time relating to members of the opposite sex. They experience a lot of personal rejection from their peers, rejection that comes with being unusually gifted and shy at the same time.

On a societal level, the cultures in which they develop also experience tremendous change. Political systems, and the philosophies they espouse, rise and wane, shaking the foundations of their respective societies. Disillusioned with what is happening in their worlds—the transitional forces at work that appear to reward a few, but oppress many—both seek refuge in nature. They seek the comfort of solitude and live alone in the wilderness—simply and close to the earth. The only way they survive is through self-denial and help from their families.

Neither marries. Both continue to be given to fluctuating, sometimes violent moods. These moods appear to be connected to what is happening in the world around them—a changing world with which they fiercely disagree. And both make it a personal mission to hurl thunderbolts of judgment upon their respective societies, railing at the forces at play in their world that are making society "go to hell in a handbasket."

And who are these two men? One is Jeremiah, the prophet of God (ca. 650 B. C.), and the other is Ted Kaczynski, the alleged "Unabomber" (1942—). Say what?!

Go ahead, take a look. It is there for the comparing. And it raises the immediate question: How did one become the outstanding personality of his age—empowering his people to survive their crises with a deeper faith in God—and the other turn out to be an accused pathological, diabolical killer? At risk of being overly simplistic, the question should be raised—and examined—because it can provide us with clues to our own capacity for good and evil and what to do about it.

II. The submitted will.

Jeremiah was submitted to the power and authority of the Holy One, while Ted Kaczynski seemingly had no authority higher than himself.

M. Scott Peck, M. D., in his fascinating book *People of the Lie: The Hope for Healing Human Evil* (New York: Simon and Schuster, 1983), refers to a pathologic orientation known as "malignant narcissism," a term actually coined by the famous personologist, Erich Fromm. Peck says this:

"'Malignant narcissism' is characterized by an unsubmitted will. All adults who are mentally healthy submit themselves one way or another to something higher than themselves, be it God or truth or love or some ideal. They do what God wants them to do rather than what they would desire. 'Thy will, not mine, be done,' the God-submitted person says. They believe in what is true rather than what they would like to be true. ... All mentally healthy individuals, to a greater or lesser degree, submit themselves to the demands of their conscience. Not so the evil, however. In a conflict with their guilt and their will, it is the guilt that must go, and the will that must win" (p. 78).

According to *Newsweek* (April 15, 1996), after Ted Kaczynski was captured by the Feds and arraigned in Helena, Montana, he was led by a group of reporters and photographers in what is known as the "perp walk." Usually, most criminal suspects, during this walk, try to cover up their faces. They hide from the lights and the media exposure. Not Kaczynski. He stared straight ahead and smirked ever so slightly, exhibiting "the smile of the smartest kid in the class."

Here is a man who has been accused of spending nearly two decades bombing innocent people he didn't know—killing three and maiming twenty-three others—in order to recreate the world in his image and likeness. Where was his guilt? Did he have any remorse whatsoever? Seemingly, these reactions were not present. At the end, all that seemed to be present in the accused Unabomber was his "malignant narcissism." He had been submitted only to himself. The smirk said it all.

III. Two statues—two philosophies of change.

In New York stand two statues across from each other on Fifth Avenue. Both are dramatic, and both have to do with world views. In front of Radio City, there stands Atlas, the mythical giant on whose straining, rippling shoulders is balanced the entire world. The expression on his face is one of intense effortfulness—willfulness at its height. Across the street, there is another figure in the facade of St. Patrick's Cathedral. It is the figure of Jesus, and the world is in his hands. Christ is holding the world—with a sense of effortlessness, securely and serenely in his tender grasp.

The image conveys the wide chasm between the way the person of faith tries to change the world and the way a destructionist attempts to change the world. The person of faith realizes, first of all, that God has saved and is saving the world—not that he or she is saving it. We are not Atlas. The world is in God's hands, not ours. Faith maintains that we are *agents* of the solution, not the solution itself. Thank God. Furthermore, the person of faith seeks the will of God *in community*, where the will of the Lord is nearly always made known, and not in the confines of self-imposed isolation. Thirdly, all efforts at world change need to be held up to the light of Scripture and the dictates of love, according to the witness of Jesus Christ.

The "Serenity Prayer" of AA goes, "God, grant me the serenity to accept the things I cannot change, the courage to change the things I can, and the wisdom to know the difference." And you wonder, if at some pivotal time in the accused Unabomber's life he had heard and internalized that prayer, would the world have been a better place because of a genius named Ted Kaczynski?

20. Spiritual Health Cures

Mark 6:7-13

⁷Jesus called the twelve and began to send them out two by two, and gave them authority over the unclean spirits. ⁸He ordered them to take nothing for their journey except a staff; no bread, no bag, no money in their belts; ⁹but to wear sandals and not to put on two tunics. ¹⁰He said to them, "Wherever you enter a house, stay there until you leave the place. ¹¹If any place will not welcome you and they refuse to hear you, as you leave, shake off the dust that is on your feet as a testimony against them." ¹²So they went out and proclaimed that all should repent. ¹³They cast out many demons, and anointed with oil many who were sick and cured them.

I. Go ye into all the world ... and give facials, and dispense aromatic hair gels.

Jesus' sending out of the Twelve seems so primitive in this modern day of avant-garde spiritual methodologies. Sending out disciples, two by two, telling folks to repent, delivering them from "unclean spirits," seems too in-your-face, unadorned, and boundary-violating. Furthermore, the admonition by Jesus for the disciples to take nothing on this missionary journey—no bread, no bag, no money; only sandals, two tunics, and a staff—comes across about as inviting as living off rolls of Communion wafers for a week.

And when you compare Jesus' way of advancing the spread of the Kingdom to the new, trendy promotions for "spiritual health," traditional Christian missionary methods seem really passé. Take, for instance, what is occurring in the spa industry. *The Wittenburg Door's* section "Not So Good News" on page 43 of the May/June issue gives us pause. Lifted from the publication *Religion Watch,* this is what compiler Brian Kelcher of *The Door* clipped:

"Physical trainers in several spas across the nation are expanding their fitness programs to include clients' spiritual health. One trainer who teaches 'aroma fitness' classes in California says: 'Sacredness is in coming together and working with each other. Everyone in my classes comes to come into alignment with their finest selves.' In some spas, clients are told that facials provide care of the soul as well as the skin. Even using an aromatic hair gel can produce spiritual insight, according to Horst Rechelbacher, CEO of Aveda Corporation. The pleasure created by the gel's scent puts users in a state of bliss, which in turn connects them with the oneness of the universe." Let the people—or the spa-goers—say, "Amen!"

II. "Eighty percent of success is showing up" —Woody Allen.

But thank God for Scripture. Thank God that we have a primitive witness in the Book, which, as Will Willimon says, "forms us, reforms us, and challenges us." Because of the witness of Scripture, even the most freed up of Christians would have a hard time turning the missionary message of Jesus into "the Gospel at La Costa." Or to make the Good News into some version of the "Sermon on the Massage Table."

But back to the theme for today: *sending out.* What Scripture discloses to us is that the very nature of the Godhead is "sending love." In John Macquarrie's language, call it "Sending Being." The God we worship is a "sending God." God the Creator/Missionary sends Jesus to inaugurate the Kingdom and rescue the world from sin and death (Jn. 3:16). Abba, the Father, in turn, sends the Holy Spirit to continue the work of Christification in the world until the end of time (Jn. 14:26). And Jesus sends out the disciples, before and after Pentecost, to spread the Good News (Mk. 6:7; Jn. 20:21). Mission, or being sent out, underlies the whole Christian enterprise—from the nature of God, to the disciples being in the living rooms of potential converts.

But what else should we learn from the nature of Christian mission? Here are some points to ponder:

A. *Mission is not Church-centered, but world-centered.* What does this mean? First of all, it means that the Church is not an end in itself, but it is God's primary means of bringing the world to Christ. Often, we in the Church get this understanding confused. We think mission should be for the sake of the Church. But the mission of God is wider than the Church. Scripture says the Gospel is to be preached to "all nations" (Mt. 28:19), and the arena in which that happens is the world. The Prophet Joel testified that God wanted the Spirit to fall "upon all flesh" (Acts 2:17), not just on the Church. Hence, the Church should be understood as the instrument of mission, not the end of it. As Archbishop Temple said, the Church is the only institution in society that should exist for those outside of it.

B. *Mission is a service and presence, as well as a proclamation.* Insofar as the Church reflects the nature of the Servant Christ, the Church has credibility. Words will take you only so far in mission; then a "sermon" has to be preached with one's feet. "Not everyone who says to me, 'Lord, Lord,' will enter the kingdom of heaven," Jesus teaches, "but only the one who does the will of my Father in heaven" (Mt. 7:21). The same could be said about the efficacy of mission. The Gospel needs to be *seen* as well as *heard*—in loving action and in service grounded in the pattern of Christ Jesus. This means that Christian mission is characterized by unmerited, or even unappreciated, service. Just as Jesus offered himself to others whether or not they responded, so should we.

Often the most effective servant-mission is simply *being present.* It is not in "preaching" or in "witnessing," or by doing the complicated or the spectacular for others. Often it is holding the Christ light out to someone just by being present to that person, allowing the Holy Spirit to work through our presence in ways that far surpass the obvious. In so doing, the Holy God, who is always present, becomes "incarnate" in the presence of the disciple. In such a witness, Jesus is exalted, and the Gospel is spread.

   C. *Mission can be an escape from self-examination and pastoral care.* To see the Christian life solely in terms of mission—as focused on others—can also be dangerous. Balance is needed. All of us know how easy it is to avoid ourselves by focusing on other people. Therefore, mission should also be a call to *spiritual depth,* not just an effort to change the topsoil of a person's or a congregation's life.

   Dr. Bob Pierce, a highly successful evangelist and worldwide missionary, and the founder of World Vision International, was speaking to a small group of clergy toward the close of his notable life. He reflected on the orphanages he had founded in Korea, on rescuing children from starvation and death in Africa, and on how he had converted thousands to Christ all over the globe. Everyone in the room was in awe of his accomplishments.

   But then Pierce surprised the group when he told them the following story: on mission gone awry. It had happened on Christmas Eve, in Stockholm, several years before, when he was traveling with the Korean Children's Choir. Pierce made a call home to his family, wishing all of them a Merry Christmas. Finally, his youngest child got on the phone. "Oh, Daddy," she said, "I wish I was an orphan so I could be with you on Christmas." Pierce broke down in tears. He realized that he had been so focused on "mission" that he had neglected the care of those closest to him.

21. No Lilliputian God

Matthew 14:13-21

[13] Now when Jesus heard this, he withdrew from there in a boat to a deserted place by himself. But when the crowds heard it, they followed him on foot from the towns. [14] When he went ashore, he saw a great crowd; and he had compassion for them and cured their sick. [15] When it was evening, the disciples came to him and said, "This is a deserted place, and the hour is now late; send the crowds away so that they may go into the villages and buy food for themselves." [16] Jesus said to them, "They need not go away; you give them something to eat." [17] They replied, "We have nothing here but five loaves and two fish." [18] And he said, "Bring them here to me." [19] Then he ordered the crowds to sit down on the grass. Taking the five loaves and the two fish, he looked up to heaven, and blessed and broke the loaves, and gave them to the disciples, and the disciples gave them to the crowds. [20] And all ate and were filled; and they took up what was left over of the broken pieces, twelve baskets full. [21] And those who ate were about five thousand men, besides women and children.

I.   Do sermonettes make Christianettes?

It's a good thing Jesus wasn't a minister today. He might still be looking for a job. How come? Because today, in the reading of the feeding of the 5,000 (at least in Mark's version of it), the text says that Jesus not only spent all afternoon *healing* the crowds of their afflictions; he also spent the whole afternoon *teaching* them as well. Therein, *gasp*, lies the rub. Jesus has done the unthinkable. He has unblushingly committed the cardinal sin of most

Episcopal churches—the sin (that is, other than doing something in bad taste) that hosts of laity are ever vigilant about each Sunday as their clergy climb into the pulpits across the nation. Jesus has preached *a long sermon*. A loooooooonnnnngggggg sermon. More than fifteen or twenty minutes, too.

For *hours*, Jesus has gone on and on. Think of the golf games spoiled. The soccer matches canceled. The tennis left undone. The gardening that goes unattended. The empty buffet lines at the club. Think of the yawns and the fidgety kids and the sore backs. Yet Jesus keeps on, hour after hour, from the high afternoon right on into the gloaming. Preaching and teaching the Kingdom. Somebody once said that sermonettes make Christianettes, and maybe Jesus knew that truth better than the rest of us who place the Word under the heel of the clock, Sunday after Sunday. Or maybe, Jesus was just gutsier than we are about taking as much time as it takes to speak the Word of the Lord. Maybe it was some of each.

II. "Miracles are not contrary to nature, but only contrary to what we know about nature"—St. Augustine.

The story says that the crowds at the end of the marathon heal in/teach in are anything but upset about having been taught for so long. In fact, they won't go away—despite being hungry, tired, and preached at. Interestingly, the text never says that *they* were hungry and wanted something to eat. It says that the *disciples* wanted them to go away and find something to eat. In other words, the disciples had had a belly full of the crowds, and they wanted relief. Relief spelled D-I-S-B-A-N-D.

Then Jesus tells the disciples not only what they do not want to hear, but what they cannot fathom as well: "They need not go away; you give them something to eat" (v. 16). Here is where we encounter the impossibility of being agents of Jesus Christ. That is why, as the disciples will do here, the first thing we do when faced with the Gospel's call to do the impossible is to seek a reasonable alternative to faith.

Let me give you an example. In 1984, a group from our small Church of the Ascension in Cartersville, Georgia, decided we wanted to start an affiliate of Habitat for Humanity—what would be the 28th in the country. We went to Americus, Georgia, the headquarters for HfH. We toured the facility. We spoke with one director after another. We saw slides of other affiliates. We saw videos of how people's lives had been changed forever through having been provided decent housing, with no interest and at no profit. We were taken by Millard Fuller's "Theology of the Hammer," believing it to be God's message to a world thirsting for love and justice. At the end of the day, our little group met with Fuller, the founder of HfH, who had taken time out of his frantic schedule to encourage us and answer any questions we might have. We were blown away.

After the small talk, one member of our group leaned forward and asked THE question: "Millard, level with us. How much money do we need before we can launch an affiliate in Cartersville?" Fuller became very serious. He leaned forward in his chair, and spoke barely above a whisper. He said, "It would be wholly irresponsible, completely negligent, totally feather-brained if you started an affiliate without at least *one dollar.* But, you have to have one dollar. Don't dare make a move without it!"

III. "Whoever believes that the All is deficient is himself deficient"—The Gospel According to Thomas.

We laughed—nervously, preposterously. He was dead serious. And what we went on to discover in Americus that day—as the disciples discovered with Jesus that evening when he told them to feed the masses themselves—is that faced with the Gospel imperative, the first thing we look for is *a reasonable alternative to faith.* We look to ourselves. To our resources. To our means and our abilities and our capacities and our wherewithal—to our five loaves and two fish. And, looking only at our strength and qualifications, which, to us, are all important, Jesus becomes unimportant. We try to be adequate without Christ.

What Jesus is telling the disciples, and what Fuller was telling us, is that the Gospel's power to feed can only be explained in terms of Jesus, not us. If the Christian life can be explained in terms of us—our talent, our treasure, our inventiveness, and not Jesus through us—then, in truth, we have little to offer anybody. And what little reasonableness we have gets used up in a hurry—about as fast as five thousand men, besides women and children, can put away five loaves and two fish.

That is why Fuller said we only needed a dollar. If we had twenty-five thousand in the bank, Jesus would be irrelevant. "Pagans," he scoffed, "needed money in the bank before they did something. Not Christians." Drop-jawed, we went on to hear him teach us about the miracle of the loaves and fish as a principle for living the Christian life—as a way of living miraculously each day. He said that the first thing that you do is not to moan about having just one dollar juxtaposed to such an enormous, capital intensive project. Don't moan or whine or carp about insufficiency—give it to Jesus. Turn it over. Surrender it. Then, as he did in the story with the loaves and fish, Jesus will take our offering and bless it. And in the blessing of it, God's power is somehow released. The "reasonable" offering becomes a "consecrated" offering. Our limited resources become God's means of unlimited grace. Possibilities beyond our wildest dreams occur. Habitat affiliates get started. Lives get changed. Freshness flowers. What we bemoan and get depressed about becomes something beyond human explanation. People are fed, and people are baffled—two common occurrences that take place when the Gospel happens.

Where, of course, the power of God becomes efficacious—when the crowds get fed, and the bafflement takes place—is the point at which the disciples *step out in faith*. Only when they take the multiplied loaves and fish to the people can they ingest this unusual form of grace. Presumably, the same power in Jesus that multiplied the food could have zapped it out to the people sitting on the green grass. But that is not the way of God. The impossible happens through the possible. The spiritual happens through the material. Jesus needed the disciples to feed the five thousand then, just as he needs us today to feed the multitudes. Not believing in our own Lilliputian resources, but in the inexhaustible power of the Gospel.

3-OEHM

22. Gospel Strangeness

Matthew 15:21-28

²¹Jesus left that place and went away to the district of Tyre and Sidon. ²²Just then a Canaanite woman from that region came out and started shouting, "Have mercy on me, Lord, Son of David; my daughter is tormented by a demon." ²³But he did not answer her at all. And his disciples came and urged him, saying, "Send her away, for she keeps shouting after us." ²⁴He answered, "I was sent only to the lost sheep of the house of Israel." ²⁵But she came and knelt before him, saying, "Lord, help me." ²⁶He answered, "It is not fair to take the children's food and throw it to the dogs." ²⁷She said, "Yes, Lord, yet even the dogs eat the crumbs that fall from their masters' table." ²⁸Then Jesus answered her, "Woman, great is your faith! Let it be done for you as you wish." And her daughter was healed instantly.

I. There is a strangeness in God's mercy.

As we all know by now, the word *gospel* means "good news." However, we might want to rename this story from Matthew's Gospel as "strange news." If in doubt, simply examine the text.

Jesus and his disciples have left Israel on their way to the beach. Their long-awaited getaway to Tyre and Sidon (comparable to modern-day Lebanon) is to take a respite from the crowds and the combative religious leaders in Israel and to take a holiday. Just as they pull the van up to the beachfront campground, and they are unraveling the hammock and icing down the beer, an unnamed woman bursts into their lives to ask for an exorcism for her daughter—and then disappears. Not that this event, in itself, is so strange.

Stranger things have occurred with Jesus and the disciples, and even stranger things are yet to come.

But there are other aspects to the story that intensify its strangeness. First, an infidel—from a geographical locale known to be wicked and godless—addresses Jesus with an expression of faith: "Son of David" (v. 22). How did that happen? Then, Jesus, normally always willing to help anyone who appeals to him in faith, comes across to this importunate woman with uncharacteristic coldness. It says that, "He did not answer her at all" (v. 23); and then he tells her: "It is not fair to take the children's food and throw it to the dogs" (v. 26).

Is this the same Jesus who fed 5,000? The same Mr. Compassion who never turned away anyone who came to him in faith? There is more. You have here also the contrast between the pagan woman's "great faith" and the "little faith" of Peter, *the leading Apostle,* which so recently caused him to sink (14:31).

II. "The one who waits for roast duck to fly into mouth must wait a very, very long time" —Chinese proverb.

So what are we to glean from the story beyond strangeness? It is reinforcement. Reinforcement of the teaching Jesus gave that unlocks the power of the Kingdom to all who use it. It is *the power in asking.* "Ask, and it will be given you; search, and you will find; knock, and the door will be opened for you. For everyone who asks receives, and everyone who searches finds, and for everyone who knocks, the door will be opened" (Mt. 7:7-8). Jesus did not say that just the chosen people who ask, or Southern Baptists who ask, or Huguenots who ask, or the born again who ask, but *whoever* asks of God receives "good things" (Mt. 7:11b).

But, strangely, it is just this "asking" that we have such trouble with. And not just with the Almighty either. It is asking for a hug. Asking for respect. Asking for commitment. Asking for time—or time off. Asking for a contribution. Asking for a promotion. Asking for a raise. Asking for equal opportunity. Asking for loyalty. Asking for a lower price. Asking for intimacy.

Why is asking such a problem? Clearly the Canaanite woman represents the kind of person who overcomes inhibitions to asking. She might well be the "patron saint of Askers." What did she overcome to get what she wanted from Jesus? Let's take a look.

She overcame the "little ol' me" myth: *my needs are not important.* "Think of all the other poor people out there who need Jesus more than I do," she could have said to herself. Or, she could have rationalized: "Jesus is BUSY. He needs to have his time away from the holy hubbub in Israel and catch his breath. I don't want him to put himself out at my expense. I'll get back to him later ... at a more convenient time."

People who have a hard time asking for what they want from the important people in their lives generally deem what *they* want to be unimportant. It is programmed into the very fiber of their being. But the payoff in having "unimportant" needs is that it relieves them of the pain of asking—and being refused. But the "faith" of the Canaanite woman rejects such belief. So what if her behavior raises eyebrows? So what if Jesus is temporarily inconvenienced? So what if the disciples get to the beach ten minutes later than they wanted? Her faith meant that her needs were important.

Barbara De Angelis, Ph. D., and author of *Real Moments,* captures the opposite of this attitude as it manifested itself in her own life: "Because my father was very rarely around and because he made a lot of promises he never kept, my experience was that if you ask, you'll be disappointed. So don't ask and take whatever you can get. For me it was beyond scarcity consciousness. It was 'I'll take the universe's leftovers.'"

The Canaanite woman also overcame the "clairvoyant" myth— that is, *Jesus should have known what she wanted without her asking.* Jesus, at various times, was shown to have the psychic capacity to know what others were thinking and feeling. However, in today's story, the Canaanite woman was not going to leave the well-being of her daughter to clairvoyance. Her request was too important for that.

Asking Jesus face to face was crucial, since, time after time, the Gospels have shown, Jesus heals people on his way to do something else. It is usually when people stop him and ask for healing—or their friends do—that Jesus directs the healing energies of the Kingdom into their lives. Without this asking, the release of God's power into that situation would not have happened.

She overcame the myth of "saintly sacrifice" too—that is, the "Christian" attitude that *others' needs are more important than my own.* Had the despairing woman lived only by the credo, "It is more blessed to give than to receive" (Acts 20:35b), she might have attained "sainthood"—but her needs would have gone unmet. Had she fallen prey to the false label of being "selfish" that is so often drummed into people—and especially women—by misunderstanding religious folk, she never would have experienced the Gospel's power to release and set free. Had she lived strictly by the belief that she was there to serve, and not to be served, she would have gone away empty—not to mention quietly resentful.

III. "If you don't ask, you don't get"—Gandhi.

In her fascinating book, *Embraced by the Light* (Placerville: Gold Leaf Press, 1992), Betty J. Eadie retells the story of what has been called "the most profound and complete near-death experience ever." Believe me, it is a spellbinding page-turner. One of the most memorable parts of the book, however, was her chapter on prayer—and how prayers were answered. She describes "many lights shooting up from the earth like beacons," which were the prayers of the people. Some were as small as pen lights, and some were no bigger than sparks. Others, however, were large, and charged into heaven like "broad laser beams."

Angels, organized to answer prayers, were streaming all over the earth from person to person, from prayer to prayer, joyously responding to each one. However, Eadie maintained, the angels always responded to the brighter, beacon prayers first—before attending to the "smaller ones," the half-hearted or insincere prayers. Even though all of the prayers were attended to in time, the deep "prayers of desire"—especially for people in need—projected straight up into heaven and were the most visible. She also saw that there was no greater prayer on earth than that of a mother for her children. These were the purest of prayers because of their sincerity and their sense of desperation. She said, "A mother has the ability to give her heart to her children and to implore mightily before God for them."

23. Who's Going to Make It?

Luke 13:22-30

²²Jesus went through one town and village after another, teaching as he made his way to Jerusalem. ²³Someone asked him, "Lord, will only a few be saved?" He said to them, ²⁴"Strive to enter through the narrow door; for many, I tell you, will try to enter and will not be able. ²⁵When once the owner of the house has got up and shut the door, and you begin to stand outside and to knock at the door, saying, 'Lord, open to us,' then in reply he will say to you, 'I do not know where you come from.' ²⁶Then you will begin to say, 'We ate and drank with you, and you taught in our streets.' ²⁷But he will say, 'I do not know where you come from; go away from me, all you evildoers!' ²⁸There will be weeping and gnashing of teeth when you see Abraham and Isaac and Jacob and all the prophets in the kingdom of God, and you yourselves thrown out. ²⁹Then people will come from east and west, from north and south, and will eat in the kingdom of God. ³⁰Indeed, some are last who will be first, and some are first who will be last."

I.   Hollywood's take on being "saved."

Throughout the stream of human history, the topic has always been popular: "Who will be saved, many or few?" It really doesn't matter from *what,* just as long as the threat is severe enough. Saved from pestilence? From famine? From global warming? From economic panic? From nuclear war? From Kenneth Starr? From hell or purgatory? All of the above arouse our curiosity beyond the level of passing interest. How many make it; how many don't? And for what reasons?

We want to know, and have wanted to know for a long time. As long as we live in a fallen, eggshell world, these questions won't go away—for think tanks, for governments, for scientists, for theologians, and for folk like you and me. These "do or die" questions make up the stuff of examined human existence, hitting as they do on the core issue of self-preservation.

Hollywood has known this for years. And 1998 is no different. First, we had *Titanic.* Who will be saved there? Next, the disaster genre gravitated away from the seas and turned toward the heavens. By late spring, the earth becomes a bulls-eye for an icy comet—code-named *ELE* for "Extinction-Level-Event"—in the film *Deep Impact.* Again, we wonder, who will be saved? when Morgan Freeman, as the President of the United States, tells the world that "Mission Messiah" has failed to nuke the comet out of existence. The result: the deadly ice-comet hurtles toward the earth—where civilization turns into an anthill of blocked freeways, suicides, and heart-wrenching good-byes.

"Who will be saved?" the viewers wonder with mounting expectation. But they will have to wait for the answer. The government turns "messiah." A special computer (what else?) selects a million people out of the country (and a male and female of each animal group) to occupy a network of underground caves in Missouri—code-named "Ark." Other than special scientists, nobody over fifty years old will be admitted. (So long, early baby boomers!) From this "remnant," which will emerge from the catastrophe two years hence, American civilization can start all over again.

So who gets saved? If you lived on the Eastern seaboard—and had not been taken to Missouri—you joined the Statue of Liberty, the World Trade Towers, the Capitol, the London Bridge, and the Arch de Triumphe—as a part of a new Atlantic coral reef. But if you lived west of the Appalachian mountains, you were saved. See the movie to find out the details ... And if that isn't enough of Hollywood's version of "who gets saved and who doesn't" for your taste, stay tuned. *Armaggedon,* starring Bruce Willis, will bring you a rocky asteroid headed toward earth—and a theater near you—this summer.

II. Kingdom participation as the settling of the score.

A hot topic for the Jews in the time of Jesus was who would be saved—and who wouldn't be—in the coming Kingdom of God. Under severe foreign domination, with little human hope for redemption, the only hope for "justice" among the righteous centered around a "judgment day" scenario. This coming Day of the Lord would descend onto world history like a comet—with similar results. The righteous would be saved; the unrighteous would not. Of course, *they* were the former, and the notorious sinners and the oppressive Gentiles made up the latter. So if justice were not apparent in the present world—and had little hope of being made apparent—the true believers needed to sit tight and hold on. At the "End of the Age," they would be vindicated by God as the honored guests at the Messianic Banquet, while the unrighteous would reap their just reward—and be cast into outer darkness with wailing and gnashing of teeth.

Jesus doesn't give an answer to the inquiring minds who were eager to know how many would be saved (Lk. 13:23). Elsewhere Jesus had said that God alone was "good" (Mk. 10:18), and that disciples of his were not to judge at all (Mt. 7:1-5)—placing judgment as to who would be "saved" or "unsaved" outside the sphere of human discernment. Maybe that is why Jesus stays silent on the subject.

But Luke cannot conclude the scene without adding one of Jesus' characteristic teachings on the subject: "Indeed, some are last who will be first, and some are first who will be last" (v. 30). Simple heredity—being a child of Abraham, Isaac, or Jacob—will not suffice, contrary to popular belief. Those who enter the Kingdom will do so from the four corners of the earth, not by pedigree, but through making a concerted choice.

III. The Kingdom within our power.

So Jesus tells his listeners, "Strive to enter through the narrow door" (Lk. 13:24). Seen against the backdrop of other teachings on the Kingdom experience, this one seems paradoxical. On the one hand, the requisite for entering the Kingdom—a state of grace rightfully called God's presence and power—is simply to become a child. To accept it as a free gift in childlike trust. Then again, the ones who experience the Kingdom are the ones who, by their conscious decision and effort, seek out God's presence and power in their lives.

In other words, nobody can "saunter" into the Kingdom of God. Nobody can get chauffeured in, or taxied in, whenever it is convenient, or whenever they get a notion to. It has to be a priority—no, *the* priority, in one's life (Mt. 6:33). That is why the "rich" have as much chance of getting into the Kingdom as a Lear jet has of landing in a bathtub (Mk. 10:25). People enter into the Kingdom in direct proportion to their neediness—and their willingness to act on their need.

So here they come. The "narrow door" people who know they have no righteousness of their own—no wealth, no prestige, no prominence, or promise—that would make them "heirs" to any righteousness of God. The only way they know to be "saved" is to surrender to Jesus. To knock single-mindedly and wholeheartedly on the door of the Spirit. They are willing to work for it, because they don't have any other option. To them and for them, the Kingdom of God becomes a present reality.

In his book, *The Parables of the Kingdom*, C. H. Dodd cites an article written by C. H. Roberts in the *Harvard Theological Review* (Vol. XLI, No. I, 1948). In this paper, Roberts argues persuasively from ancient papyri and other sources that the expression *entos humon* (in the context of "the Kingdom of God is *among you* or *within you*" [Lk. 17:20-21]) is most accurately translated: "the Kingdom of God is *in your hands,* or *within your power.*" If that indeed is the case, the paradoxical nature of Jesus' teaching on the Kingdom comes clear.

Yes, the Kingdom is a gift for all, but what determines whether it is *within our power* is whether or not we experience it, whether we choose to place ourselves under the Kingdom's power and grace. That is why only the ones who ask, and keep on asking, receive. Why only the ones who seek, and keep on seeking, actually find. And why only those who knock, and keep on knocking, have the door of the Kingdom opened to them (Lk. 11:9-13). These "last" will indeed be "first."

24. Open Up to Life

Mark 7:31-37

³¹ Then Jesus returned from the region of Tyre, and went by way of Sidon towards the Sea of Galilee, in the region of the Decapolis. ³² They brought to him a deaf man who had an impediment in his speech; and they begged him to lay his hand on him. ³³ He took him aside in private, away from the crowd, and put his fingers into his ears, and he spat and touched his tongue. ³⁴ Then looking up to heaven, he sighed and said to him, "Ephphatha," that is, "Be opened." ³⁵ And immediately his ears were opened, his tongue was released, and he spoke plainly. ³⁶ Then Jesus ordered him to tell no one; but the more he ordered them, the more zealously they proclaimed it. ³⁷ They were astounded beyond measure, saying, "He has done everything well; he even makes the deaf to hear and the mute to speak."

I.   "Ephphatha. Be opened."

The Gospel of Jesus opens people up. The poor are opened to hope. The captives are released. The blind see. The oppressed—in mind, body, spirit—or in society—go free (cf. Lk. 4:18-19). Whoever you are, in whatever way you are locked up, or closed off, when the Kingdom Jesus gives comes upon you, openness ensues. In fact, it's as if you can't simultaneously experience the "jubilee of Jesus" and be locked up for long.

So the "deaf and dumb" man from the Decapolis is brought to Jesus for healing—to be "opened," as it turns out. Whereas, in so many healings Jesus performed, the faith of the person is commended, the text for today never mentions that the man with a speech and hearing problem wanted to be cured—or that he had any faith to be cured. It only says that an undesignated "they" brought him to Jesus, and importuned Jesus to lay his hands on him. Whatever "faith to be healed" was on hand, most likely Jesus or "they" had it. Not the deaf-mute.

This should be an important learning for the Church's ministry of healing. Often the person who is experiencing great trial or suffering—especially physical sickness—does not feel like praying at all. "Faith" might be the furthest thing from this person's heart or mind. At that point, *the faith of the community,* the believing "theys," hold up to the Lord those who need prayer for healing. The suffering person, through intercessory prayer and the steadfast love of the community, receives the healing power of God, regardless of her or his "spiritual condition."

On an obvious and important level, the story reveals one of the most poignant moments in the healing ministry of Jesus. By privately pulling the man aside to minister to him, Jesus shows his sensitivity as a healer. *Care* concerns him just as much as *cure.* Furthermore, Jesus shows why he could be called a "shy Messiah." There will be no whiff of ostentation in what he does. Only reserved tenderness. Here, and throughout the healings of Jesus, there are no bright lights, no TV cameras and commercial breaks, and no 800 number prayer hotlines at the bottom of the scene to pad a mailing list. Compassion, not notoriety, will be the motivation for doing the works of God. To make the point even clearer, Jesus here orders the crowd to tell no one what happened.

Nothing from the text indicates the etiology of the man's speech and hearing problems. Stacy Davids, a clinical psychologist doing graduate work in New Testament studies, has endeavored to define medical diagnoses of many of the people Jesus healed. She has concluded that this identification process works better in cases of "organic disease" (wounds, lesions, hemorrhages) or "functional disorders" (heart disease, high blood pressure, cancer). In the former, the tissue of the body is damaged; and in the latter, the malfunction of one part affects the whole.

But in the case of "personality disturbances" the diagnosis is much harder. The "unseen" made itself known through the "seen." Illness was not so much the result of a malfunctioning physical process as it was an indication that one's being—spiritual, physical, and/or social—was somehow out of alignment. Who can say for sure what caused the man's problems? The good news is that you don't have to know what is wrong with you before you can get well.

II. California "peering."

Another way to interpret the story of "Ephphatha" concerns not just the healing of this isolated individual's speech and hearing blocks, but the "healing" of a broader "blockage"—our own.

From a vivid childhood memory, Maya Angelou offers a powerful contrast between this state of "locked-upness" and that of "openness" (in *Wouldn't Take Nothing for My Journey Now*, New York: Random House, 1993). The story concerns Angelou's Aunt Tee, a member of her extended family living in Los Angeles: "She was seventy-nine when I met her, sinewy, strong, and the color of old lemons. She wore her coarse, straight hair, which was slightly streaked with gray, in a long braided rope across the top of her head. With her high cheekbones, old gold skin, and almond eyes, she looked more like an Indian chief than an old black woman."

She had retired and lived alone in "a dead, neat ground-floor apartment. Wax flowers and china figurines sat on elaborately and heavily starched doilies. Sofas and chairs were tautly upholstered. The only thing at ease in Aunt Tee's apartment was Aunt Tee." One day, she was telling Angelou about her work as a housekeeper for a wealthy couple in Bel Air, California. Aunt Tee oversaw a fourteen-room ranch house that also had a day maid to clean, and a gardener to tend the lush gardens.

Even though Aunt Tee fixed the couple and their guests wonderful three- and four-course dinners, she watched them grow more isolated and leaner. After a few years, the couple stopped entertaining altogether. Every night they would sit in a "dry silence" as they ate their evening meal of soft scrambled eggs, melba toast, and weak tea. Aunt Tee said that while she saw them growing old and withdrawn, she didn't see herself aging at all.

In fact, she was quite the social maven. She started "keeping company" with a chauffeur down the street. On Saturdays, Aunt Tee would cook a pot of pigs' feet and a pot of greens, fry chicken, make potato salad, and bake a banana pudding. That evening, her chauffeur friend and another couple would come over, and they would eat and drink together, and then play records and dance the night away. During all this revelry, "jokes were told, fingers snapped, feet were patted, and there was a great deal of laughter."

One merry Saturday night, Aunt Tee was startled by what she saw. She and her friends had been playing cards when she looked up and saw her employers—the wealthy couple—looking in on them through the cracked door. A little peeved, Aunt Tee laid down her cards and went to the door. The couple backed into the hall, and said: "Theresa, we don't mean to disturb you, but you all seem to be having such a good time ... We hear you and your friends laughing every Saturday night, and we'd just like to watch you. We don't want to bother you. We will be quiet and just watch."

Aunt Tee said that she saw no harm in agreeing, and she talked it over with her company. Amazed and amused, they agreed. And so they watched Aunt Tee and her friends "live it up." Angelou said that the story had stayed fresh with her for nearly thirty years: the closed-up rich couple contrasted with the less well-to-do open merrymakers. Life had closed in for the former; the latter displayed a love of life, an ability to take great pleasure from small offerings, and a deep awareness that the world owes you nothing—that every gift is exactly that, a gift. Pray that the Gospel would open us to this kind of rich wisdom day by day.

25. Tracking the "Real" Jesus

Mark 8:27-38

27Jesus went on with his disciples to the villages of Caesarea Philippi; and on the way he asked his disciples, "Who do people say that I am?" 28And they answered him, "John the Baptist; and others, Elijah; and still others, one of the prophets." 29He asked them, "But who do you say that I am?" Peter answered him, "You are the Messiah." 30And he sternly ordered them not to tell anyone about him. 31Then he began to teach them that the Son of Man must undergo great suffering, and be rejected by the elders, the chief priests, and the scribes, and be killed, and after three days rise again. 32He said all this quite openly. And Peter took him aside and began to rebuke him. 33But turning and looking at his disciples, he rebuked Peter and said, "Get behind me, Satan! For you are setting your mind not on divine things but on human things." 34He called the crowd with his disciples, and said to them, "If any want to become my followers, let them deny themselves and take up their cross and follow me. 35For those who want to save their life will lose it, and those who lose their life for my sake, and for the sake of the gospel, will save it. 36For what will it profit them to gain the whole world and forfeit their life? 37Indeed, what can they give in return for their life? 38Those who are ashamed of me and of my words in this adulterous and sinful generation, of them the Son of Man will also be ashamed when he comes in the glory of his Father with the holy angels."

I.   The real Jesus, and a fooled retriever.

On one level, the question about who Jesus is couldn't be more irrelevant. With mortgage debts to service and car notes to pay, with kids to raise and jobs to keep and relationships to maintain, with retirement to save for, with cancer or heart disease or AIDS to stay free of, with NATO being expanded and the Dow Jones Industrial Average rollercoasting—who, really, spends much time wondering about (or caring about?) the question: "Who do people say that I am?" (Mk. 8:27). Not many.

For most of us, this little incident that occurred with Jesus and his closest disciples some 2,000 years ago, in an area north of Galilee known as Caesarea Philippi, seems as far away as the Pathfinder on Mars. Think about it. When was the last time you heard the word "Messiah" mentioned at a cocktail party, or at a business meeting, or saw it written up in *Better Living?*

On another level, however, the subject couldn't be more relevant. "Who do people say that I am?" has become a question of Alpine proportions—not only inside the Church, but outside of the believing community as well. Leading the charge of renewed interest in Jesus from the "outside" is Robert Funk, the founder of the Jesus Seminar. Funk, a Guggenheim Fellow and former Fulbright Scholar, has set himself to the task of engineering a long overdue "prison break" for Jesus. His purpose? To loose the chains of a Jesus who has been kept for two thousand years in the jail of orthodoxy, and to bring him into the sunshine of historical reality and contemporary thinking.

So in his controversial book, *Honest to Jesus: Jesus for a New Millennium* (New York: HarperCollins, 1996), Funk emancipates Jesus from what he calls "creedalism." Put simply, when it comes to Jesus, *Nicea has very little to do with Nazareth.* The Jesus that the Creeds profess and the Church exalts as "Lord and Messiah" is little better than a "Gospel cover-up" for the real guy. The historical Jesus—Funk's Jesus minus Church chains—needs to subvert the "Christian" Jesus by giving him a swift "demotion."

With all the passion of a streetcorner preacher, Funk maintains that the "religion of Jesus" has been twisted into the "religion *about* Jesus." Rather than going after what Jesus saw, heard, and sensed was so powerful and mesmerizing about the "domain of God," the Church instead opted for "faith in Jesus." The Church substituted the *agent* for *the reality to which the agent pointed*. The proclaimer became the proclaimed, meaning that the "Christ of faith" overpowered the "Jesus of history."

Funk wastes little time throwing down the gauntlet before "a pious America that is overweight on dim self-righteousness." Like Jesus himself using a scene from everyday life to convey an unseen truth, Funk uses the following image to illustrate the malady of the misguided masses who desperately need his new Jesus for a new age:

"The fellow who runs the granary down the street in the industrial park where my office is located frequently plays 'fetch the ball' with his dog. Every so often he will pretend to throw the ball and then, while the dog is looking away, he will actually throw it. Because the dog has not noticed this deception, he sits patiently at his master's feet and waits. His master points in the direction of the ball. The dog, not understanding the meaning of that gesture, barks at the pointing finger.

"The first and many subsequent followers of Jesus are like that dog: Jesus points to some horizon in his parables, some fabulous yonder, something he called God's estate, which he sees but to which the rest of us are blind. Like dogs, we bark at the pointing finger, oblivious to the breathtaking scene behind us. All we need to do is turn around and look" (p. 10).

II. Is God's foolishness underappreciated at the Westar Institute?

Funk contends that instead of looking to see what Jesus saw, his disciples stared at the pointing finger like the retriever in the story. And the majority of Christians ever since have been doing likewise. But, away from the authoritarian structures of denominations and out from under the ecclesiastical constraints of seminaries, the crusade to remove the Church's "self-serving doctrines" about Jesus is being carried by the "sound thinking" religion departments of secular institutions.

What is the nature of Funk's new "altar call" for the new Jesus, and for the new age? Funk answers: Jesus was a charismatic visionary. He was a poet of the Kingdom of God, a subversive sage, intent on cavorting with all sorts and conditions of "insalubrious types." Jesus sat in taverns and took his meals with swindlers and prostitutes and untouchables—in effect, saying that fellowship with God was completely free and unmediated by any religious institution. Jesus' primary claim to fame was that "he caught a glimpse of what the world is really like when we look at it with God's eyes," Funk says. As an enlightened teacher, his sole mission had nothing to do with "incarnating God" or being a "blood sacrifice." He taught of God's domain, and called followers to "celebrate life, to suck the marrow out of existence, to explore and probe ... without the fear of a tyrannical and vindictive God."

Funk, and his Jesus Seminar-ians, have done the Church a great service. Their radical scholarship has been a kind of "No-Doz," or a cup of cold water flung in the face of a "drowsy" Christianity. But what Funk forgets in his insistence on orchestrating the "prison break" of Jesus are two things that the episode at Caesarea Philippi teaches us.

A. *Faith is a gift of the Holy Spirit.* Without this gift-like knowledge, Peter cannot say what he says. And Jesus cannot be known as "Lord and Messiah" (Acts 2:36). "Blessed are you, Simon son of Jonah!" Jesus tells Peter. "For flesh and blood has not revealed this to you, but my Father in heaven" (Mt. 16:17). Only by God's grace can Peter, or any Christian, confess that Jesus is Emmanuel, or "God-with-us."

B. *Jesus as "Messiah" can only be discovered in the community of believers.* Faith in the uniqueness of Jesus' relationship to God—this one-of-a-kind indwelling—comes from people who saw him, heard him, and experienced what he did. The ones they told, in turn, had something of the same kind of experience happen to them. The confession of Jesus as Messiah emerged, in each case, from a "personal discovery" of Jesus as authoritative for faith. This revelation can never be "forced" on them; God always leaves us the freedom to deny and disagree. That is why the mystery of the Incarnation will not be "grasped" in think tanks, or in the cathedrals of the "wise and intelligent." But it will be revealed to "infants," according to God's gracious will (Lk. 10:21).

26. The Dishonest Businessman

Luke 16:1-13

¹Jesus said to the disciples, "There was a rich man who had a manager, and charges were brought to him that this man was squandering his property. ²So he summoned him and said to him, 'What is this that I hear about you? Give me an accounting of your management, because you cannot be my manager any longer.' ³Then the manager said to himself, 'What will I do, now that my master is taking the position away from me? I am not strong enough to dig, and I am ashamed to beg. ⁴I have decided what to do so that, when I am dismissed as manager, people may welcome me into their homes.' ⁵So, summoning his master's debtors one by one, he asked the first, 'How much do you owe my master?' ⁶He answered, 'A hundred jugs of olive oil.' He said to him, 'Take your bill, sit down quickly, and make it fifty.' ⁷Then he asked another, 'And how much do you owe?' He replied, 'A hundred containers of wheat.' He said to him, 'Take your bill and make it eighty.' ⁸And his master commended the dishonest manager because he had acted shrewdly; for the children of this age are more shrewd in dealing with their own generation than are the children of light. ⁹And I tell you, make friends for yourselves by means of dishonest wealth so that when it is gone, they may welcome you into the eternal homes. ¹⁰Whoever is faithful in a very little is faithful also in much; and whoever is dishonest in a very little is dishonest also in much. ¹¹If then you have not been faithful with the dishonest wealth, who will entrust to you the true riches? ¹²And if you have not been faithful with what belongs to another, who will give you what is your own? ¹³No slave can serve two masters; for a slave will either hate the one and love the other, or be devoted to the one and despise the other. You cannot serve God and wealth. "

I. "Wisdom consists in the anticipation of consequences" —Norman Cousins.

Florence, Colorado, at first glance, seems to have little in common with Jesus' tale of the dishonest businessman. Maybe at a second glance, too. But this town is the home of the "Supermax," a 190-million-dollar correctional complex referred to by some as "the Alcatraz of the Rockies." Here, the "worst of the worst" serve out their time—such notables as Theodore Kaczynski, the Unabomber; Timothy McVeigh, the Oklahoma City bomber; and Ramzi Yousef, the World Trade Center bomber.

Contrary to what you might expect, in an Associated Press release on the Supermax, things don't appear too grim for these super-villains. For instance, after spending the better part of three decades in a cramped cabin by himself in the rough Montana wilderness, Kaczynski now has his own shower, toilet, electric lamp, desk and stool, cigarette lighter, and a 13-inch TV. His cell, the article reports, is slightly larger than his cabin, and it is climate controlled. He can order all kinds of books—from novels to law texts—from the extensive library at the Supermax, and have them hand-delivered to his cell. Kaczynski can also choose his daily fare for breakfast, lunch, and dinner from several options on the prison menu. Plus, Kaczynski and the others receive freshly laundered bed linens, as well as their prison khakis, three times a week.

Maybe if the crooked manager had known that such a "correctional" opportunity awaited him after cooking the books on his boss, he would not have made such a guileful effort to cut under-the-table deals with his boss's creditors. Not that he ever would have made it to the Supermax. Cookers of books don't end up in Florence, Colorado. Most of them, at least first-time offenders, take their "striped sunshine" in one of those low-security, publicly traded correctional facilities that cater to "white collar" criminals—

you know, where tennis is offered along with the library and fitness facilities.

But this rogue does not relish the prospects of jail—much less the dreary alternatives of "digging" or "begging." He is not content with a personal future determined by someone else—be it a foreman on a construction site, or some almsgiver out on the streetcorner. Those options just won't do. So, taking a cue from the motto of the Christopher Society—"It is better to light a candle than to curse the darkness"—the crafty steward clings to the only straw he has. He cheats the landowner one more time by summarily reducing the substantial debt his "subs" owed him. In this way, the crafty con-man prepares for a future he can live with.

II. A follower of Jesus is not to become "idle as a painted ship on a painted ocean."

"You shall not steal" (Ex. 20:15), God makes clear to Moses and the Hebrew people on Sinai. And so we listen to the outcome of Jesus' story expecting a major-league conviction for the dishonest manager. But then comes more than an "unexpected twist" on the story—it is a jaw-dropping, gasp-bringing outcome that puts ants in the pants of every upstanding, law-abiding person who hears it. The master does not call the police. Does not call for a full-scale investigation of the foxy steward. Does not call the DA, or his accountant, or the Better Business Bureau to black-ball the steward from ever doing business there again. He *praises* the double-dealing schmuck. He *lauds* the sly, slippery steward for his foresighted action—regardless of his unscrupulousness, or whether or not he repents and makes amends for his unprincipled behavior.

What's going on here? What does Jesus seem to be saying? *Pious people can become so "spiritual" that they are of no "earthly" use.* They can set out to avoid "sinning" to such a degree that they never get around to doing much good for anyone else. As they try, in effect, to be more spiritual than God, the world which God loves reaps no benefit from their "savedness." Caught up in their love for "sweetness and light," these fastidious folks end up, in Samuel Taylor Coleridge's words from *Rime of the Ancient Mariner:* "idle as a painted ship on a painted ocean."

"Virtue herself is her own great reward," wrote Silicius Italicus, but Jesus questions the notion. What good is virtue if sought for its own sake? Self-glory? Self-honor? Self-goodness? Jesus is not personally interested in these goals, as if he believed they could be attained (Mk. 10:17-18). Virtue needs to be spent—for the sake of others. Sanctity for self alone turns squalid, and makes for saints with a smell.

The Kingdom person Jesus lauds is not "perfect." He or she is not simply someone who keeps a 4.0 moral average with God. The Kingdom person is not a *perfectionist* but an *entrepreneur*. The person who is radically open to God's working through her or him in all sorts and conditions of ways is, at the same time, fully in touch with the ways of the world outside. Such a person sees opportunity—the convergence of Gospel love and worldly need—when it comes along, and then pursues it with *realness:* real gladness and real singleness of heart. And yes, real imperfection.

III. Faithful in "very little."

Babe Ruth was once heard to say, "Never let the fear of striking out get in your way." And even though Ruth was the home-run king of baseball, he also topped the strike-out category. Still, he was never paralyzed by the fear of failure. He did not suffer "paralysis by analysis" (or by excessive virtue). One wonders to what degree this attitude enabled Ruth to be such an extraordinary player. One wonders to what degree the people of God could be more effective by taking this fearless, emboldened attitude toward the life God calls us to live.

Most "saints" exist in fairy tales and in myth (often revised and edited). Maybe that is where they should stay. On this side of the grave, we need to live by grace—and our wits. Conversion is not simply from the neck down, but also from the neck up. To live with the confidence that God is somehow working through us, even in our mistakes, sets the Christian free to soar. Even in the tawdriness of our moral instability and wayward ways, God's providential grace is occurring. That is the affirmation of a faith that means something not only to God, but also to the world.

In closing, where is this "faith" lived? Mostly in the "small things" of life, in the day-to-day world. As Fred Craddock has incisively written in his commentary on Luke: "Most of us this week will not christen a ship, write a book, end a war, appoint a cabinet, dine with a queen, convert a nation, or be burned at the stake. More likely the week will present no more than a chance to give a cup of water, write a note, visit a nursing home, vote for a county commissioner, teach a Sunday school class, share a meal, tell a child a story, go to choir practice, and feed the neighbor's cat. 'Whoever is faithful in a very little is faithful also in much'" (Lk. 16:10).

27. As Much of God as You Want

Matthew 5:1-12

¹When Jesus saw the crowds, he went up the mountain; and after he sat down, his disciples came to him. ²Then he began to speak, and taught them, saying: ³"Blessed are the poor in spirit, for theirs is the kingdom of heaven. ⁴Blessed are those who mourn, for they will be comforted. ⁵Blessed are the meek, for they will inherit the earth. ⁶Blessed are those who hunger and thirst for righteousness, for they will be filled. ⁷Blessed are the merciful, for they will receive mercy. ⁸Blessed are the pure in heart, for they will see God. ⁹Blessed are the peacemakers, for they will be called children of God. ¹⁰Blessed are those who are persecuted for righteousness' sake, for theirs is the kingdom of heaven. ¹¹Blessed are you when people revile you and persecute you and utter all kinds of evil against you falsely on my account. ¹²Rejoice and be glad, for your reward is great in heaven, for in the same way they persecuted the prophets who were before you."

I.   Salvation on the mountain.

If you want a mesmerizing, out-of-the-ordinary read, try Dennis Covington's *Salvation on Sand Mountain: Snake Handling and Redemption in Southern Appalachia* (New York: Penguin Group, 1995). Covington, a novelist and teacher of creative writing at the University of Alabama at Birmingham, who also writes on the South for the *New York Times,* became involved with snake handlers when he covered the trial of a preacher in Scottsboro, Alabama. The preacher, the Rev. Glenn Summerford, in a drunken rage, had given his wife two ghastly alternatives. Either he would shoot and kill her, or she would have to stick her hand into a box of his church's rattlesnakes—and let the pit vipers do the job for him.

Darlene Summerford had chosen the second option. Repeatedly, her husband made her stick her hand in the box, and each time she was bitten by a rattlesnake. Miraculously, before Darlene succumbed to the snake venom, Glenn passed out, and Darlene made her way to a neighbor's house. The ambulance and the police were called. Darlene lived. Glenn, who carried a previous record of convictions for grand larceny, got life in prison under Alabama's Habitual Felony Offender Act.

The seedy happenings of the Summerford case are not the point here. There is a lot more to the "communion of the saints" than the twisted religion Covington uncovered in Scottsboro. But while Covington was continuing his investigation into the snake handlers, he was approached one day by Charles McGlockin. A man in his early fifties, with "a full head of dark hair, and hands the size of waffle irons," McGlockin, who lived modestly in a house trailer in New Hope, Alabama, had preached on the radio, at county fairs—even out of the back of his '72 Chevy van as he crisscrossed the South. Seeing a new soul to win, he came up to Covington and handed him his card which read: "End-Time Evangelist."

Looking him in the eye, McGlockin went right to the point: "Mister, you can have as much of God as you want. These seminary preachers don't understand that. They don't understand the spirit of the Lord. They're taught by man. They know the *forms* of godliness, but they deny the *power*."

We all know that McGlockin couldn't get his big toe inside any diocesan Commission on Ministry—for plenty of good reasons. But ironically, the End-Time Evangelist puts his finger on something wholly pertinent to this feast celebrated on the Sunday After All Saints' Day. Those followers of Christ who have gone on "from strength to strength in the life of perfect service"—those exemplars of the faith that we celebrate today—*all wanted more of God than most*. And, accordingly, they received more of God than most. Like the blessed in the Beatitudes, they experienced a hunger for God that the world could not touch, and this hunger comprised the means of their infilling. They knew the Gospel, in Rev. McGlockin's words, less as a "form of godliness," and more as the life-blood of their very existence. They could not live without Christ as their Source and as their purpose for living.

But their desire for the power and love of God did not make them plastic, sinless automatons. Nor did they fall prey to "paralyzing virtue"—what Fred Buechner describes as the terrible side-effect that besets people who consider themselves morally superior to others. If anything, these all-too-frail, clay-footed human beings knew the depths of their own corruption—an awareness that deepened as they continued to grow in grace.

Still, despite the ongoing persistence of their imperfections, "grace abounded all the more." Paul could write Timothy that he himself was foremost among sinners (1 Tim. 1:15). Luke could write that Mary Magdalene was possessed of seven devils before Jesus healed her (Lk. 8:2). Augustine could speak honestly of his jaded prayer life: "Give me chastity and continence, but not now." Young Francis would take many years before he would "come to himself" and discard his life as a model of rebellion in his hometown of Assisi.

II. The "pilgrim fare" for saints.

Yet it is not so much these notables of the faith that we esteem today. Already they have their dates on the Christian calendar. It is the rank-and-file followers of the Lord—known and unknown, seen and unseen—that make up that great cloud of witnesses, of Christians that we celebrate on All Saints'. Aunts and uncles, teachers, friends, family members, coaches, clergy, and unnumbered others all of whom have played their special part in drawing us into the "blessed company of all faithful people," we hold up in thanks and praise for their witness. Since the Gospel is communicated most effectively *relationally* rather than just *propositionally*, we can testify that without their steadfast love and undimmed faith, the Gospel in all of our lives would have gone, if not un-heard, then probably unheeded.

One such person is William McElwee Miller, a most remark-able, but largely unheralded twentieth-century "saint." In a book entitled *Francis: A Call to Conversion* (Grand Rapids: Zondervan, 1988), authors Duane Arnold and George Fry refer to Miller as an example of a "saint" who simply followed the path of Jesus and allowed himself to be used as an instrument of God's peace. He grew up in the mountains of Virginia in the early part of this century, and went to seminary at Princeton. He then spent fifty years as a missionary in Iran. Stories have abounded about Miller, one of which was that he walked the full five hundred miles from Mashad to Tehran—rather than burden his donkey.

Another story about Miller concerned the time he was travel-ing along the border of Iran and Afghanistan. Along the way, he encountered a Muslim sage. Together the missionary and the mullah rode along the narrow path that divided the countries. Inevitably, they began to speak about each other's faith. The Persian asked the Presbyterian, "What is Christianity?" To which Miller replied, "It is like a journey. For that trip I need four things—*bread,* for nour-ishment; *water,* for refreshment; a *book,* for direction; and *opportu-nity,* for service. These are my pilgrim fare. Jesus provides me with these things. I trust him on my way. That is Christianity."

I would add an additional item to the "pilgrim fare" Miller mentions. That is a *community,* for support, correction, and care. And, in reality, that is what All Saints' comes down to. This "com-munion of the saints" is not about an exalted group of self-spiritu-alized people, but about a community of people who, for better or worse, set out to follow Christ amid the complexities and compli-cations of a fallen world. A community, in other words, called out for service in the name of Jesus—despite tarnished lives and chinked haloes—to live the Gospel until the Lord comes again.

28. Running on Empty

Matthew 25:1-13

Jesus said, ¹"Then the kingdom of heaven will be like this. Ten bridesmaids took their lamps and went to meet the bridegroom. ²Five of them were foolish, and five were wise. ³When the foolish took their lamps, they took no oil with them; ⁴but the wise took flasks of oil with their lamps. ⁵As the bridegroom was delayed, all of them became drowsy and slept. ⁶But at midnight there was a shout, 'Look! Here is the bridegroom! Come out to meet him.' ⁷Then all those bridesmaids got up and trimmed their lamps. ⁸The foolish said to the wise, 'Give us some of your oil, for our lamps are going out.' ⁹But the wise replied, 'No! there will not be enough for you and for us. You had better go to the dealers and buy some for yourselves.' ¹⁰And while they went to buy it, the bridegroom came, and those who were ready went with him into the wedding banquet; and the door was shut. ¹¹Later the other bridesmaids came also, saying, 'Lord, lord, open to us.' ¹²But he replied, 'Truly I tell you, I do not know you.' ¹³Keep awake therefore, for you know neither the day nor the hour."

I. The marriage feast: the biggest deal in town.

Since there was no cable TV to entertain, no Six Flags Over Jerusalem to excite the masses, no NFL or NBA to stretch over half the year, no rock concerts or philharmonic symphonies to attend, no children's sports activities to take up whole weekends, and no eighty-hour work weeks to be enslaved by—a simple wedding celebration was among the highest of times in a Palestinian village at the time of Jesus. It is little wonder that when Jesus looked for symbols to point up the joy of the Kingdom experience, he likened it to the joy and celebration of a wedding feast.

Exegetes are inconclusive about the exact nature of the wedding protocol of a Palestinian wedding at that time. Generally, however, we can assume that the Parable of the Bridesmaids concerned the final stage of the marriage. There *were* marriages of attraction, but usually the "engagement" was arranged between both fathers months before the ceremony. The "betrothal," in which vows were exchanged and the groom made payments to the father of the bride and gave the bride a special wedding gift, had already taken place. By being betrothed the couple was considered "legally" bound to one another, without living together. The wedding itself, however, took place months, maybe a year, after the betrothal. And the feast ordinarily was held in the fall after the harvest.

The exact features of a wedding party are hard to pinpoint. According to the best data, the bridegroom, accompanied by his companions (Mt. 9:15), went to his bride's home. After receiving her parents' blessing (cf. Gen. 24:60), the young bride—veiled and surrounded by her attendants—joined the wedding train that went to the groom's paternal home for the wedding. For some reason, there always seemed to be a long delay in the wedding party's procession to the bridegroom's house.

Was it a host of last-minute details that needed attention? Did one of the partners get "cold feet"? Did the premarital agreement need to be reworked? Who can say? Who hasn't done a wedding where the scurrying went on until the last minute?

Palestinian customs at the turn of the twentieth century seem to verify a slightly different protocol—one that is more nearly in sync with the parable for today. Here the groom, delayed by dealing with contractual matters with his parents-in-law, arrives at a late hour at his paternal home, where his bride, with her bridesmaids, wait for him. At that late hour, the marriage would take place, and the merrymaking begin.

II. The haves and have-nots.

The message of the parable, however, is not about the manners and customs of Palestinian weddings. It is an allegory emphasizing the theme of being ready for the return of Jesus—the coming Bridegroom-Lord—despite the apparent delay. The bridesmaids, of course, represent the Church. Although all ten appear to be prepared, five were foolish, and five were wise. What distinguishes the wise from the foolish is not that they fall asleep waiting for the bridegroom. Both do that. The difference is that the former "have oil" when they wake up, while the latter do not.

What is pertinent here is that having oil is what counts when the great consummation comes. You can't run to Sam's, or to the local Exxon, or over to K-Mart to find this "oil," because it is the "oil of faithfulness." You can't acquire it from anyone else, but only as a by-product of your relationship with God and neighbor. Asking someone to borrow his or her share of this oil would be as ridiculous as asking someone to be baptized for you—it just won't work. Personal decision is required.

Jewish traditions had long spoken of "oil" as a symbol of a living faith that issued in good deeds, and this "oil" was what comprised effective preparation for the return of the Lord. This is *not* idly watching the heavens for the end to come (cf. Mt. 25:31-46). Readiness, or "having oil in your lamp," is living the Gospel life for today in expectation of tomorrow's glory yet to be revealed.

What is worth examining in light of the parable are the things that we fall prey to that leave us "on empty." The attitudes or events or modes of living that diminish our capacity to "have oil" in our lamps. Of course, there are a host of possibilities to explore. Here are two.

A. The Ahab syndrome. Melville's classic folk epic reveals the tragic disintegration of a once heroic whaleman, Captain Ahab, who becomes obsessed with the god-like pursuit of the great white whale, Moby Dick. Ultimately, Ahab's obsession does him and his crew in, as Moby Dick destroys everyone under Ahab's charge except Ishmael. This "Ahab syndrome" seems increasingly to exert a more pervasive kind of "spell"—one our world finds itself under today. Spawned in part by the current emphasis on specialization, it means that we are being consumed with one aspect of our living at the expense of all others. It may be work. It may be exercise. It may be making money—or worrying about it. It may be trying to be perfect. It may be an addiction to drugs or alcohol or food or sex. It may be sports—or a child's sports program. It may be doing churchy things. It may be the internet, or high-tech wizardry. Whatever the fixation, the result is that we get hooked on patterns of behavior that spiritually destroy us. This complex leaves us "without oil." I am convinced that one reason so many "believers" do not make it to church on Sunday morning is because of the Ahab syndrome operating in their lives. On Sunday morning, there is not enough "oil" present to get them out of bed and into the fellowship in any kind of meaningful way.

B. The absence of "vision quest." One of the fascinating characteristics of the American Plains Indians has been their insistence on taking time to wander. They chose to be alone in nature, to be present to the Divine in the natural world, seeking to discover more clearly who they were, and what the Spirit of God was beckoning them to become. The Hopi Indians had a term for this kind of spiritual discipline; it was called "vision quest." It involved a retreat into nature that promoted *spiritual discovery*. During this time—much like the time Jesus spent in the desert to discern his true vocation as Messiah—these Native American "questers" would set about to open new pathways for God to speak to them, away from their everyday world. It was at this time that they would re-map themselves spiritually. Gaining new insight, they would commit themselves to the truth that had been revealed to them. In this way, their lives stayed fresh and creative. They kept the "oil" in their lamps.

It is possible that "vision quests" are going on all over the place in the Christian Church. But the nearest example of a "vision quest" happening to somebody I know concerns a fifty-year-old, hard-working, overweight, over-Scotched, almost-divorced physician who went on an Outward Bound trip with ten strangers for a week in the Rockies—compliments of his family. He came back a different person.

Not only had he lost fifteen pounds, and not only had the sparkle in his eye returned, but he had discovered something more: The "wisdom of the world" he had been living by was an empty lamp. The oil of grace could only fuel his new future.

29. The Painful Parable

Matthew 25:14-15, 19-29

Jesus said, [14] *"For it is as if a man, going on a journey, summoned his slaves and entrusted his property to them;* [15] *to one he gave five talents, to another two, to another one, to each according to his ability. Then he went away.* [19] *After a long time the master of those slaves came and settled accounts with them.* [20] *Then the one who had received the five talents came forward, bringing five more talents, saying, 'Master, you handed over to me five talents; see, I have made five more talents.'* [21] *His master said to him, 'Well done, good and trustworthy slave; you have been trustworthy in a few things, I will put you in charge of many things; enter into the joy of your master.'* [22] *And the one with the two talents also came forward, saying, 'Master, you handed over to me two talents; see, I have made two more talents.'* [23] *His master said to him, 'Well done, good and trustworthy slave; you have been trustworthy in a few things, I will put you in charge of many things; enter into the joy of your master.'* [24] *Then the one who had received the one talent also came forward, saying, 'Master, I knew that you were a harsh man, reaping where you did not sow, and gathering where you did not scatter seed;* [25] *so I was afraid, and I went and hid your talent in the ground. Here you have what is yours.'* [26] *But his master replied, 'You wicked and lazy slave! You knew, did you, that I reap where I did not sow, and gather where I did not scatter?* [27] *Then you ought to have invested my money with the bankers, and on my return I would have received what was my own with interest.* [28] *So take the talent from him, and give it to the one with the ten talents.* [29] *For to all those who have, more will be given, and they will have an abundance; but from those who have nothing, even what they have will be taken away.'"*

I. This is justice?

The Parable of the Talents is a hard story for our modern world to take in. First, there is the whole imagery of master/slave that is not only antiquated, but so antithetical to love and everything we believe about human dignity. Next, our sense of justice—that is, the sense that everything needs to be as equal as possible—gets slammed up against the wall when one slave gets five talents from the master, another receives two, and another just one. Even though each slave receives according to ability, the inequality of it sticks in our throats. How is that fair? The story ends hitting a major nerve in our society—the growing disparity in our culture in which the rich get richer and the poor get poorer (Mt. 25:29). How is that fair? Verse 30 ices the cake of uneasiness, when it speaks of the master hurling this poor, one-talent slave into outer darkness forever and ever—merely because he put the money in safe deposit instead of putting it all in a small-cap mutual fund that earned 25% more than the S&P 500 that year. Is *this* Good News? Hello?

The Parable of the Talents is also a hard story to hear because it brings up for each of us not *those things done,* so much as *those things left undone.* Those things that we know we should have been doing, but have put off, either out of procrastination, or to pursue other safer, more prudent undertakings. The parable brings up, as well, that sense of envy we may feel toward *those who have done better with their talents than we have with ours.* Whether or not we doubt that our Master is returning to us for an accounting, as the one in the parable does, we know that the hourglass of our lives is inexorably spilling sand from the upper to lower section. This makes the parable take on even more force and immediacy—at least for "boomers-on-up."

II. "To life!"

"In this book," says Henri Nouwen, "I want to tell the story of the cup, not just as my story, but as the story of life." And Nouwen does so beautifully in his work *Can You Drink the Cup?* (Notre Dame: Ave Maria Press, 1996). Nouwen cites the passage from Matthew (20:20-23) in which the sons of Zebedee, with their *mother* leading the way, come to Jesus with a request. The mother (of these two grown men) asks Jesus to promise her that her two sons may sit to the left and right of Jesus in the coming Kingdom. To James and John, Jesus replies: "You do not know what you are asking. Are you able to drink the cup that I am about to drink?" (v. 22). They say that they can, an answer Jesus accepts; but he denies the request about preferential seating, deferring to the Father, who alone can decide such matters.

Nouwen, inspired by this text after a morning Eucharist he himself celebrated at the Dayspring Chapel in Toronto (where he lived with and ministered to men and women with mental disabilities), reflected on drinking *this "cup of life" that Jesus calls his followers to drink.* He found that it involved three processes: *holding*, *lifting*, and *drinking*. These three processes are also involved in the creative expression of our talents—for to express our giftedness for the sake of the Kingdom is to "drink the cup" of Jesus.

A. HOLDING: Nouwen says that before we can drink our "cup," we must first "hold it." And "holding it" means to own it— to know what is there, usually through disciplined effort and risk-taking. But to realize what we are called in our uniqueness to do with our lives is "to drink the cup of Jesus."

Although potentially exhilarating, this task is not easy. Our creativity wants out, but we sense a harsh world waiting either to ignore it, or to shame it out of us. Elizabeth O'Connor, in her masterful work *The Eighth Day of Creation: Gifts and Creativity* (Waco: Word Books, 1971), provides a solution. She says that one of the primary purposes of the Church is to help the faithful discover their gifts, to enable each one of us to "hold" what is in our cups. Citing the example of her own parish—The Church of Our Savior in Washington, D. C.—O'Connor says that this "holding" happens in community, in small sharing groups, where one's giftedness can be identified, confirmed, and supported. The small urgings, dreams, and creative intimations of the Spirit can only be discerned by a common listening and a vulnerable sharing. In such a safe place, a person's often "secret" or "buried" talents can be "held." Here, away from a doubting world of "sameness," uniqueness can be discovered and owned—timidly, at first, but then confidently, with a growing boldness that comes with stepping out in faith.

B. LIFTING: "Lifting the cup is an invitation to affirm and celebrate life together," Nouwen writes. And the best example of a toast, to illustrate the point Nouwen draws from the Hebrew, is *"L'chaim"* (to life!). Living our giftedness is our "toast" to God and the world; it is our way of saying "to life!"

"Lifting" also involves our making a commitment to our giftedness. In lifting the cup, we commit to expressing in our lives what the cup holds—publicly, in front of God and the world. O'Connor speaks to the side-effects of this lifting: "Somehow if I name my gift and it is confirmed, I cannot 'hang loose' in the same way. I would much rather be committed to God in the abstract than to be committed at the point of my gifts. ... If I develop one gift, it means that others will not be used. Doors will close on a million lovely possibilities. ... Commitment at the point of my gifts means I must give up being a straddler ... my commitment will give me an identity, but I do not like the sound of this. I do not want to be boxed in ... I would rather keep the quest for who I am on a more 'spiritual plane'" (pp. 42-43). Lifting, in other words, means taking responsibility for the living of our gifts—and for making the sacrifices necessary for them to grow.

The reality of what "lifting the cup" involves should break us out of the fantasy best expressed in a *New York Times Book Review* a few years back. There was a cartoon by H. Martin that pictured a word processor clicking away by itself while the author stood at the door calling to his wife, "Edna, come quick! I've got a book that is writing itself!"

C. **DRINKING:** "The cup that we hold and lift we must drink," Nouwen declares. And what he means is that we must embrace—drink—what life brings to us when we "hold" and "lift" the cup of our lives to a thirsting world. Both the blessing and the pain are in the drinking of the cup. "Somehow we know that when we do not drink our cup and thus avoid the sorrow as well as the joy of living, our lives become inauthentic, insincere, superficial, and boring. We become puppets moved up and down, left and right by the puppeteers of this world. We become objects, yes, victims, of other people's interests and desires. But we don't have to be victims. We can choose to drink the cup of our life with the deep conviction that by drinking it we will find our true freedom" (p. 83).

And that is the reward that "drinking the cup" brings. As it says in the parable, we "enter into the joy" of the Master (v. 23b). The joy of co-creating with God redounds to us. We feel alive and free. We grow potent and full of self-respect. As O'Connor says: "The reward will not be in higher wages, another rung on the ladder, the acclaim of our peers, but in the creative forces which flow within us and accomplish in our own lives the gracious work of transformation."

30. A Litmus Test of Faith

Matthew 25:31-46

Jesus said, ³¹ *"When the Son of Man comes in his glory, and all the angels with him, then he will sit on the throne of his glory.* ³²*All the nations will be gathered before him, and he will separate people one from another as a shepherd separates the sheep from the goats,* ³³*and he will put the sheep at his right hand and the goats at the left.* ³⁴*Then the king will say to those at his right hand, 'Come, you that are blessed by my Father, inherit the kingdom prepared for you from the foundation of the world;* ³⁵*for I was hungry and you gave me food, I was thirsty and you gave me something to drink, I was a stranger and you welcomed me,* ³⁶*I was naked and you gave me clothing, I was sick and you took care of me, I was in prison and you visited me.'* ³⁷*Then the righteous will answer him, 'Lord, when was it that we saw you hungry and gave you food, or thirsty and gave you something to drink?* ³⁸*And when was it that we saw you a stranger and welcomed you, or naked and gave you clothing?* ³⁹*And when was it that we saw you sick or in prison and visited you?'* ⁴⁰*And the king will answer them, 'Truly I tell you, just as you did it to one of the least of these who are members of my family, you did it to me.'* ⁴¹*Then he will say to those at his left hand, 'You that are accursed, depart from me into the eternal fire prepared for the devil and his angels;* ⁴²*for I was hungry and you gave me no food, I was thirsty and you gave me nothing to drink,* ⁴³*I was a stranger and you did not welcome me, naked and you did not give me clothing, sick and in prison and you did not visit me.'* ⁴⁴*Then they also will answer, 'Lord, when was it that we saw you hungry or thirsty or a stranger or naked or sick or in prison, and did not take care of you?'* ⁴⁵*Then he will answer them, 'Truly I tell you, just as you did not do it to one of the least of* *these, you did not do it to me.' ⁴⁶And these will go away into eternal punishment, but the righteous into eternal life. "*

I.   The King and I.

There are no parallels in any of the Gospels to Matthew's portrayal of the Last Judgment. Here we uncover Jesus' last words in his last discourse—an apocalyptic climax Matthew has carefully set out to construct. It is the culmination of a theme Matthew has emphasized repeatedly in chapter 25, one that has been stressed on the last two Sundays previous to today's Christ the King Sunday.

The theme could best be summarized in the Greek word for "watch" or "keep watch" *(gregoreo).* The word literally means "to have sleep taken away"; but the way Matthew uses it, the word's message carries a much more active, productive meaning than sleeplessness. It means "be awake to opportunity." Be awake to the opportunity that the coming of the exalted Son of Man presents—whether it is in entering the marriage feast, or in the multiplying of your talents, or in having the opportunity to love the "least of these" in your midst. This is crucial, because if you miss being awake to the opportunity God is presenting now, you will miss out on experiencing the ultimate in blessedness: the Kingdom "prepared for you from the foundation of the world" (25:34). And to miss that opportunity, Matthew states emphatically, is tragic.

II.   The Christian Essential: Radical Monotheism.

One thing that can be said about Jesus is that he lived and moved and had his being among the social strata of his day that could aptly be called "the least, the lost, and the last." In a world that valued prestige ahead of money, Jesus refused to acknowledge any "social ladder." He dined with political traitors. He touched the diseased and those considered unclean. He broke social taboo by esteeming women—even going so far as to openly converse with a *Samaritan* woman. His last-will-be-first-and-first-will-be-last attitude horrified those who harbored any pretensions to absolute rightness. Jesus made it clear that he was not only unimpressed by ancestry, wealth, authority, education, or virtue; he considered these "status trophies" to be *stumbling blocks* so significant that it would be easier for a camel to get through the eye of a needle than for the "rich" to enter the Kingdom experience (Mk. 10:17-25).

What lay behind this righteousness to which he called his followers—a standard that exceeded that of the "scribes and Pharisees"? Out of what sense of freedom could he act so cross-tribally, cross-culturally, and cross-theologically? The late Carlyle Marney, in his work *Priests to Each Other* (Greenville: Smith-Helwys, 1991), called this "the Christian Essential." He said that some have designated this essential as "love" or "humility" or "compassion" or "justice." Marney said that Jesus had more in mind than simply instilling an ethic or forming noble character traits in his followers. The "essential" was a relationship. This relationship is what Richard Niebuhr termed "radical monotheism."

Marney quoted Niebuhr from the latter's book *Radical Monotheism and Western Culture* (New York: Harper & Row, 1960) as saying: We are, in the Gospels, impressed not that Jesus loved, or that he was humble, or that he was merciful. It was that he loved the Father. He loved God radically, and God he radically obeyed. He pointed out that 180 verses in the Gospel of John alone are in the context of this obsession. There is no legitimate way to talk about Jesus Christ apart from this radical monotheism.

"We are not called to love our neighbor as we love God, but as we love ourselves. We are to love God as we love nothing else. The Church rests on this. Mercy, justice, compassion, humility? These all proceed from the love of the Father. Everything in Christianity stems from this."

Niebuhr's wisdom is well worth noting here, lest we turn the criteria for the Sheep-Goats judgment scene into meaning only how successful we have been at Christian-do-goodism. That is not our obsession, though sometimes it seems that way. Augustine may have had the answer. All of us know the great Christian thinker's famous dictum—"Love God and do what you will." But everyone else except Augustine has forgotten what he added and asked in the same breath: "What do I love when I love God?"

And that question establishes the essential that underlies the faith-in-action theme of our reading for today. When we love "the least"—when we feed the hungry, when we give the thirsty something to drink, when we welcome the stranger, when we clothe the naked, when we care for the sick, and when we visit the prisoner—we do so *because every self is an incarnation of Abba-God.* Every self is a member of Abba's family, which means that every self is precious, *every self is Jesus.*

Therefore, the "radical monotheism" relationship, which forms the essential of our faith, summons us to love Abba *in others.* Freely. Unconditionally. Unself-consciously—not to be considered a "good Christian" or a "good citizen." As someone pointed out, often the more "respectable" we get, the less redemptive we become! We love, in other words, not because the "least of these" deserve it, or appreciate it, or are changed in character by it. We love because the nature of Abba is being formed in us through the Spirit to express the life of Christ Jesus in the givenness of our lives. If we don't, we remain just "skin-deep" disciples, and that is tragic.

III. The "acid test" of a living faith.

Walter Rauschenbusch, the great spokesman for the "social gospel" at the turn of the century, maintained that the true test of an individual's—or of a community's—religious experience was *their commitment to change the social wrongs in God's world.* He said that people may grow worse by getting religion—more judgmental, more self-righteous, more deluded, more rigid, and more unresponsive to human need. As a proof text on the danger of religion, he cited the passage in which Jesus spoke of "scribes and

Pharisees" who "crossed sea and land" to make a single convert that became "twice as much a child of hell" as they were (Mt. 23:15). It's hard to miss his point.

But what Rauschenbusch was getting at was that mission to a broken and banged-up world was the "acid test" of a living faith. *Who we are in relation to those around us* reveals the depth of our faith. This faith is not a possession—something we have, like an insurance policy, or a suit of clothes. It is not a faith that is a set of propositions—a litmus test as to where one stands on abortion or same-sex marriages. It is not a faith that consists of dos and don'ts that justifies the believer as righteous. This faith, down deep, is about something that one *is*. A *being* faith, lived in a world that needs to think more in terms of *us*, not *them*.

A little Hasidic tale makes this point beautifully, and is worth ending on. Rabbi Shlomo said: "If you want to raise a man from the mud and filth, do not think it is enough to keep standing on top and reaching down to him with a helping hand. You must go all the way down yourself, down into the mud and the filth. Then take hold of him with strong hands and pull him and yourself into the light."

Afterword

In 1987, after ten years as a parish priest, I had sensed that God wanted me to change directions. To write—and to do so from the position of my primary responsibility as a priest. That "call" was fine, except that I also wanted to eat. And I had a hunch that my family wanted to eat too. What was I to do?

Necessity might as often prove to be the "mother of invention" in the Church as anywhere else. It was for me. The solution flowered at a seminar on desktop publishing that Nynex Corporation and Aldus put on in Atlanta. I could see after the seminar that typesetters were going the way of Noah's ark after reaching land—they were history. Anybody could publish material with a computer, so why not produce a publication, based upon the Episcopal Eucharistic Lectionary, that would assist clergy in the often lonely, yet exhilarating, task of preaching every week?

A survey by the College of Preachers in 1987 provided the hard data I needed to convince me that this kind of publication was needed in the Episcopal Church. In effect, the survey said that clergy loved to preach, but felt overwhelmed by the process of getting there. Sunday was not a day of rest for them. And the remainder of the week was even worse. They needed help. And if they needed help, their parishioners needed help too—believe me. Surviving a lousy sermon ain't no fun.

And so, fresh from earning a graduate degree from the School of Theology at the University of the South, Sewanee, Tennessee, I turned to three of my favorite teachers as possible contributing editors in their respective fields: Howard Rhys in Scripture; Don Armentrout in Church History; and Sue Armentrout in Church and Culture. They jumped at the opportunity, and Sue Armentrout suggested that the publication be called "Synthesis," since Anglicanism rests on a "synthesis" of Scripture, Tradition, Reason, and Experience.

The name *Synthesis* worked, and we were off to the races. Susan McLeod, a gifted liturgist and parish musician from the Church of the Ascension in Cartersville, Georgia, came on board as the "Worship" editor. Isabel Anders, a fine writer with exceptional editorial skills, also joined our team as Managing Editor.

I took on the "Experience" component of the Anglican Quadrilateral, and ended each week's issue with "Postscript," a page-long piece that dealt not so much with what the Scripture *said* as what it *says*.

Synthesis, more than I ever dreamed possible, took off. Nearly 550 issues have been produced for subscribers—mainly in the United States—over the last ten years. Other subscribers are in Canada, the Philippines, Honduras, France, and Kenya—even Tasmania. The outreach has extended around the world.

Synthesis has also spawned several other publications, including *Synthesis CE*—a lectionary study curriculum—and three books: *Understanding the Sunday Scriptures: The Synthesis Commentary, Years A, B,* and *C.*

I have been cajoled for several years by lay subscribers to bring out a collection of my "Postscripts" as a book. *Between the Lines: Reflections on the Gospels Through the Church Year* is the result of their importunity.

I would love to hear from you, the reader.

Please write me at: P. O. Box 11428, Chattanooga, TN 37401.

For more information about other Synthesis materials, please contact: kkthorne@erols.com, or call 301-352-5504.

Lectionary Readings
Included in the Chapters

1. Advent 1-B
2. Advent 4-B
3. Christmas Day—Annual
4. Epiphany 1-C
5. Epiphany 2-C
6. Last Epiphany-B
7. Ash Wednesday—Annual
8. Lent 1-C
9. Lent 3-C
10. Lent 5-C
11. Palm Sunday-B
12. Easter Day-B
13. Easter 3-B
14. Easter 4-C
15. Easter 6-C
16. Day of Ascension—Annual
17. Day of Pentecost—Annual
18. Trinity Sunday-C
19. Proper 7-A
20. Proper 10-B
21. Proper 13-A
22. Proper 15-A
23. Proper 16-C
24. Proper 18-B
25. Proper 19-B
26. Proper 20-C

27. All Saints' Day—Annual
28. Proper 27-A
29. Proper 28-A
30. Christ the King Sunday-A

Scripture quotes are from the New Revised Standard Version, 1989.

p124 prop like beacons of
light — Embraced By The Light